There are four sections of this book

1- Preparing for the journey; opening and following the roadmap of a spiritual path
2- Facing the dangers and challenges of the road
3- Navigating the road of life
4- A collection of road trips.

Some may be disappointed with the direction I've taken with this book. Some will wish I had kept it generally spiritual without a focus on one faith. Some will wish I had kept it Christian, and not specifically Catholic. I hear you. Early on in my spiritual journey I would have agreed with you. Please know I love and respect all people, including all sincere spiritual seekers and followers of God.

This where I'm coming from. I believe, and science has proven that on the deepest level of existence, we are all connected. We are all here on this earth together. All social organisms (families, schools, teams etc.) need a leader to fulfill their purpose. Only one person in all of history ever claimed to be humanity's leader: Jesus Christ. He proved that Kingship by His teaching, miracles, and most of all by lovingly giving His life for us. No other spiritual teacher has done what Jesus did and the only group and religion that can trace itself back directly to Jesus Himself is the Catholic faith and Catholic Church. I have no elitism in me, and again, I respect everyone who gives their life to God. I believe God is always more interested in what you are willing to do; than what you say you believe. I also know Jesus is the one who lifts up all sincere spiritual seekers and lovers of God, life and others to the Creator.

The Fast Lane

In this book, I'm presenting the spiritual life, not as a life that is dull or half dead as it is often considered; but life lived truly free, and to the fullest. You may or may not be very happy and comfortable with your life right now; but no matter what you're at as you read this, there comes a time in everyone's life when all that we attained up to that point is not enough; not the comforts and pleasures, not the popularity or recognition, not the security or achievements. We discover that none of it will be enough to give us the sense that our life is worth living. Maybe you have already tasted it: the emptiness of so much of modern life and wondered: is this all there is? The truth is that God makes each of us with a hole inside that only He can fill. We spend our lives exploring things that we hope will fill the hole, only to discover that they don't. It's time to change lanes.

I'm looking at our life journey as a three lane highway.

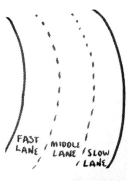

The lane to the right, is the *slow lane*. It is where people go, who are not moving very quickly; either because they are just getting on, or about to get off, or they are just very cautious. In the slow lane, the game of life happens TO you. You're not really in control, you're just kind of going along for the ride.

In the *middle lane* people are moving quicker than the slow lane. In life, this lane is packed with those who are playing the game of life for their own advantage and/or amusement.

All of us start out in life traveling the slow and middle lanes. We were all once helpless human infants and children; born into this world completely vulnerable and unable to take care of ourselves. Our whole focus was how to get the big people up there to take care of us. "Don't forget about me! I'm down here, and I'm little, and I can't do very much. Don't forget to feed me, to change me, to keep me safe, healthy and warm. I'll do anything to make sure you don't forget me. I'll be cute; I'll cry; I'll scream. *Don't forget about me!!!*" You can't blame a little one. If you were to say to them "You're just a selfish piece of garbage!" that would be ridiculous. That's a child.

However an adult is supposed to be someone who can see beyond themselves, and not be limited to their own immediate physical and social needs. Someone who knows how to look and live beyond their own immediate interests and enrich the lives of others. Using this definition; I guess it becomes obvious that many adults have never grown up, and are stuck in the middle lane. Many even doubt that there is a third lane, because all they have ever seen is people that play the game or have the game played on them.

There *is* more. There's another lane; as untravelled as it may be. The third lane is the *Fast Lane*. On a real highway, those in that lane are the ones who are really moving; passing the people moving slower in the other two lanes. I'm not saying the quality of life is to be judged by speed. The *Fast Lane* is where people are really living; freed of the manipulation and control games; living in the Holy Spirit; living life beyond the game. They are in the world, but not of the world.

(Some highways have a fourth lane called an HOV (High Occupancy Vehicle) lane. I guess correlating it to the spiritual life; in life these are the ones who are REALLY traveling with the angels and saints!).

We spend portions of our lives in all 3 lanes. No one lives in only one, and they are all necessary in driving, and in life. We all have downtime when we just need to relax and take it slow. We also have times when we have to function in the world. I also believe most people have a taste of the spiritual life with and for God that is *Fast Lane* living.

Think about what lane you spend most of your time in, and how well is that working for you as you navigate your way through life. My hope is that this book will motivate and empower you to live more in the *Fast Lane*. Those who know me know that I like to do things differently- so **Before you go any further: jump ahead and read "The Fathers Love Letter" on page 124-5.**

The whole book; the whole life with God is really based on the Love expressed in this letter.

GOD IS GOOD ALL THE TIME

Section 1
Getting your vehicle ready for the journey

Just a few questions

As you start out on this journey: Do you love being you?
Do you love your life?
Are you afraid to die?

Whether you are going on a trip in a car, motorcycle or bicycle, before you set off you have to make sure your vehicle is ready. It has to be functioning properly for it to be a good trip. The engine and transmission have to working right. Tires have to be inflated. You have to have enough gas. Faith, spirituality, and religion can help a person be ready for, and be able to travel the road of life.

Rosemary

Rosemary is the adorable little girl in the video I use to open up my retreats. If you haven't seen her, you can watch it on Youtube: "Rosemary in Heaven". It's hard to not smile or even laugh out loud, as you

9

watch her enjoying every moment with her bubbles. Battling cancer and chemotherapy, Rosemary was abandoned by her family once she came down with the disease; and yet here she is so alive and full of joy. Why do I open up my retreats and now this book with this little girl? Because she is showing us: this is what it looks like when a person has the spirit of God strong in them. How much of what you were able to see and feel is alive inside this little girl is alive inside you? *And how hungry are you for more?* Many, especially young people, think spirituality and religion are boring. I'll give you this- *a lot of religious people are boring*. But having the Spirit of God alive in you, the *Fast Lane*, is the good stuff that every person dreams of, and knows in their soul they were born for.

You might be thinking: "why is he making a big deal out of this? She's an innocent little girl. She doesn't know any better." *She knew.*
She *knew* her body wasn't working right. She *knew* the medicine was making her more sick. Rosemary spent the whole morning throwing up. It took her until afternoon to get up the strength to get out of bed. She *knew* her family wasn't coming around anymore. The day before I filmed this video, was family visit day. I was playing with Rosemary, and she noticed another little girl her own age laughing and playing with her mommy, and she cried, because she didn't have that love anymore.

And yet in the moments I captured on the video; she chose, that with that bottle of bubbles; and some idiot with a video camera (namely me) to have as much fun as possible. *Do you live like that?*

I met this boy in Nicaragua, walking through his village with a cake on a tray. I loved watching him because he was really enjoying himself. It was like he was the mayor; like he owned the place. He was smiling, saying hello to, joking and talking with everybody. I admired his lively spirit and struck up a conversation. He told me his life story:

Every morning of his life since he was four years old; his mother makes a cake; puts it on the tray, cuts it up into pieces, and sends him out, telling him not to come home until it's dark; or he had sold the whole cake.

It appeared to be a very poor village that he lived in. I got the sense people didn't have money for food, never mind cake. There was also no electricity; so when it gets dark, everyone goes inside. He had never sold the whole cake, and never had a day off to just play.

I bought the entire cake and gave away a piece to every child in the village. I gave him the money, and said "now you can go and play." He had his first day to just be a kid, and play for a few hours. I saw that he had the same big smile on his face as when he was selling the cake. His happiness did not depend on whether he sold the cake or not. It came from inside. He just loved his life, no matter what he was doing.

Could *you* find joy in the middle of a hard life like that? *This what I care about!*

I really don't care
I don't care about how much your house is worth.
I don't care whether you live in a gated community, or are reading this in a jail cell.
I don't care what kind of car is in the driveway.
I don't care whether you're on the honor roll of your school, or employee of the month at work.
I don't care how many trophies or awards you have received in the course of your life.
I don't care how smart your phone is or whether you have the latest ipod or any other technology.
And I care even less whether you twit, tweet, tumble or how many friends you have on Facebook.

What I care about is:
Do you get up in the morning;
jump out of your bed saying:
"I'm here. I'm happening. Let's go!!"?
And if not: why would you want to live like that?

Have you noticed this?
When you wake up in the morning, you truly have no idea what the heck is going to happen that day. You can't control most of what the world is going to throw at you.

Why do I bring up control? So much of the pain I have seen people inflict on themselves and each other is the result of the inability to deal with the reality of not being able to control everything, or even very much of what happens to them.

I also bring up control, because this is a book about growth; and the more we all grow in wisdom and maturity, the more we are expected to be in control. It may not have been that long ago that you couldn't feed yourself; or couldn't wipe yourself. (I pray you have those two things worked out by now! If not, don't worry- it will come to you.)

The one thing you *can* control is: how you label yourself and the experiences of your life; and the Holy Spirit gives you the ability to see and label yourself and your life with the eyes of faith.

Check the label
How can you label yourself?
You're somebody's son or daughter.
You're a member of a family.
You're member of a community.
You're a student of a school or an employee.
You might be a member of a team or another kind of group.
Who you are *more than anything?*
You are a woman or a man of God.

How alive is that identity inside you? More than anything, that will affect the whole rest of your life.
How much do you live that reality (the Fast Lane)?

One of the ways I like to get people thinking about labeling is to show my rock. Over the years I have visited many rock stores. (I know you're thinking-"He's cool; rock stores!"). When he was little, one of my nephews was into collecting rocks. I don't know why- maybe he was psycho or something. But he was a smart little boy, figuring out from listening in on conversations between me and his father, my brother; that his Uncle Tony is the traveller in the family. He added up in his little brain that maybe I travel to places where they have rocks he didn't have. So he would always plead with me, that whenever I saw a rock store, would I please pick him up something.

I once found myself passing a place claiming to be the largest rock store on the planet, and I figured: "I Guess I better buy the kid a rock". They truly had what seemed like millions of rocks in there; but it was this ugly one here that caught my attention. My first reaction was: "who would be stupid enough to buy something this ugly?"

(I know; I did.)

It gets worse. I look at the price tag underneath and it said $33.00 for a pair of them. I'm thinking: "what kind of drugs do you have to be smoking to look at this rock and say- "oh that's a bargain, I better grab that!") I'm saying to myself "these people are crazy". It caught my curiosity about why was it so expensive; and it didn't take me long to realize that some mental midget had displayed the rocks on the wrong side.

I'm not a big rock expert, but I know this: if you want to sell your rock; you show people this side not the other.

I bought the pair of them. One half I gave to the kid; and the other one, ever since, I have used on practically every retreat that I do. There are several messages:

* don't judge a book (or a rock) by it's cover
* the beauty & value is on the inside
* and my biggest reason for using the rock is about the choice. I have a choice about which side I will display and focus on; and that will affect how I feel and act towards the rock. This is true with ourselves and life as well.

*

There have been many stories in the news demonstrating this. The eighth grade students in a town upstate New York alerted the police that one of their classmates was going to pull "a Columbine". *(Several years ago, 2 teenaged boys put on black trench coats, brought bombs and guns to their school and set out to kill a lot of people. Their school was called Columbine and ever since then, if a student is going to shoot up their school, that's what they call it).*

Even though this boy was only thirteen; the police took it serious. They broke into his house and found the trench-coat, and all the bombs he built. He was in the middle of trying so buy some guns. They busted him; and put him in a mental jail.

Soon after the incident, I'm doing a Confirmation retreat in that town, and I remembered the news story. I also realized that the students on the retreat were the same age as the boy in the incident, and I asked if any of them knew him. A lot of them did. When the incident happened, the media said that he was an outcast; that he was bullied, rejected, ridiculed. I asked the students on the retreat if that was true, and they all agreed that it was.

Have you ever been in a situation where other people acted like they didn't want *you* around? Where *you* were the one who was disrespected, bullied, made fun of, or left out? If you have been through that; you know how much it can hurt.

I learned that after being released, he came back to his town. The bullying got worse, and he took his life. That young man took all his pain, and stuck on the ugly side of the rock, *he* was going to do something ugly with it to hurt others, and then himself.

There is another way to label and deal with pain in life. By seventeen years old Killian Mansfield had already become a professional level ukulele player. (Why someone would want to get so good at that at such a young age I have no idea.) In his teen years; he was diagnosed with a rare incurable disease, and was told that he did not have long to live. Can you imagine being that young and handed a death sentence like that. That's Killian's story.

When he found out he was going to die soon; he came up with an idea: to record a CD of himself on the ukulele with professional musicians in a music studio.

His plan was that after he was gone, they could sell the recording to raise money to help other kids who came after him, who had the same illness.

Killian lucked out. Because of all the places to live, he was from the Woodstock area; famous for probably the biggest and best rock concert ever. Apparently a lot of the musicians liked it up there and never went home, so Killian got to record with some of the most tal-

Cover of Killian's CD, available on the internet. I bought it to show my support. Maybe you can too.

ented musicians in the country. He writes on the inside cover of his CD: " Cancer is just a disease. It doesn't get to decide who I am or how I deal with feeling sick."

I will always respect Killian; he took *his* pain, and *he* did something beautiful with it.

As I write these words, I am praying for, and have only one thing in my heart: "that through this book, you will come away shining brighter in the Holy Spirit than you ever were before".

Why am I so confident it will apply to you?

Because every single one of us were made for this.

I know, not everyone in the world believes that.

Many people think it's only certain people that are meant to be close to God. That it's only a privileged few who can travel in the *Fast Lane.*   **It is not true.**

Every person that God makes; He makes with the capacity to be alive with His Holy Spirit. Is this the planet you live on; where everyone you meet is shining bright?

Obviously not!

We are in a world where most people are living on the ugly side of the rock. The United Nations says that on this planet more than 1 out of 3 people is seriously depressed. Their studies also reveal that at least another 1 out of 3 people is addicted to something. That means 2 out of 3 people on this planet are not free. They are controlled by their depression or by their addiction.

The news among young people in the United States is even worse. The U.S. is the most affluent and advanced culture in all of human history; and yet as I write this book, in this society 1 out of 100 young people has an eating disorder. 40% of young people cut themselves. The third biggest reason why young people die in America is being killed by another teenager. The second biggest cause of teenaged death is suicide. The number one reason is accidents (cars, guns, drugs); but most law enforcement officials will tell you that when it comes to teenagers; a lot of the accidents are really suicides. The way the law works though; is that if there is no proof, like a note, they can't legally call it a suicide, and young people overwhelmingly don't leave messages behind. The police will not investigate either; the family is upset enough that their child is dead. They won't go to them and say "we're going to investigate, we think they took their lives". Still the police believe that the real biggest reason we lose our young is that they take their lives. How heartbreaking is that?

People ask me all the time: "Tony why do you run around speaking to hundreds and hundreds of groups a year; two and three groups a day; without making anything for yourself?" Because the amount of pain in this world is breaking my heart; it's killing me that I got to grow up in a world, where the biggest reason we lose our young people, with their whole lives ahead of them, is that they take their lives. It's because I believe that the Creator means for us to live here way better than we do.

Now, if God made everyone to be shining bright with his Holy Spirit, and living lives of peace, love, joy, freedom, courage, strength and integrity; how did we end up with a planet where most people are so miserable and destructive?

To summarize most of the answers we could come up with it would be: ***it's the way people have dealt with the way God has set things up.***
The juvenile prison that I volunteer at every Friday is not very attractive at all. I offered to bring in some pictures; and was told I could only bring in one. I decided on this one because it's the whole Catholic, Christian faith in one picture: ***Jesus knocks at the door of our hearts***. I'm sure you can see Jesus and the door; the heart might take a second look- the middle of the heart is above
Christ's head and the two arches extend from there.

Christians, Catholics believe that the most important thing about this reality is that the love of the Creator of all of this is here. Not everyone believes that. Atheists, don't believe there is a Creator. Some people believe there is a Creator; but that He doesn't get involved; that He kind of sets everything in motion and then cuts out and says "see you later". Christians, Catholics believe this is ridiculous. Everything we know from life is that anybody or any thing you created out of love, you want to be close to.

The love of the Creator is here, and it is not just floating around the universe. Our faith is anchored in a personal relationship. God reaches out to love you personally. ***Right this second and every moment you will ever live; He's knocking at the door of your heart. Do you know what that means?*** It means you were not an accident. You were not a mistake. You may have been a surprise; but no matter how your parents felt about it when you were born; God meant for you to be here, and He meant for you to be you. He loves you!

So Jesus is knocking at the door of your heart. You may have noticed that the door has no door knob or door handle; meaning that "the door of your heart can only be opened by you". God can do whatever He wants; but the *one thing He won't do*: force Himself on you. He loves you so much He didn't make you a robot. He won't push His way into your life. He respects yours, and everyone else's freedom to let Him in, or slam the door in His face. It's up to you.

What's wrong with the world you are living in? You're living on the earth at a time of tremendous human advancements; and most people are full of themselves. They're full of what they know, what they can do, what they have accomplished, and what they have accumulated. They've slammed the door in His face.

Ask yourself: how open is the door to *your* heart? If you were to meet Jesus right now, would you melt into His arms? *And if not;* whatever did you allow to become more important than that? *And* what would it take for you to change this?

Maybe you are doing very well with Jesus. Maybe you are close to Him and accepting His love, and following Him is the center of your life. Maybe you feel close at times; but other times not so close. Maybe up to now you have had nothing going on with God at all. It all depends on the openness of your heart, and *all of us* have further steps to take on this journey with God.

When you read the Gospels (the part of the Bible where Jesus is actually walking and talking) it will amaze you how many times Jesus uses the word "Heart". You begin to understand who Jesus is; and what His mission is: *to disarm and to jump-start the human heart.*

The open heart, the acceptance and welcoming of Christ is the key to the fast lane, the journey of, and with God. You can park yourself in a church building 24-7. You can memorize every line of the Bible from front to back. But if you never open up your heart; embracing a deeper, greater love, you will never understand what the Catholic, Christian faith is all about, and you will not ever be traveling in the *Fast Lane.*

(A person's emotional life is meant to be intimately connected to their life with God; but feelings are not the only indication of how close you might be to God.)

What opens up a human heart?

There are a number of things that can do that.

1- *The beauty of God's creation.* In the film *"In the Shadow of the Moon"* several of the astronauts who got to go into space talk about how the beauty of creation they witnessed caused them to grow in faith. God has wired us in such a way that to be immersed in the wonders of what he created touches the soul; but some people live in some pretty ugly (and sometimes smelly) places.

2- *Pure love.* Some people have someone in their life that they have never worried for a moment might reject them. Some even have someone they know would die for them. That's the way God loves: with no conditions or limits. God's love has nothing to do with how much we receive, appreciate or reciprocate that love. Not everybody gets that kind of love; just ask many of the young people I meet in jail.

3- *Miracles.* Some people will always believe; because there was something in their family or their life that made them feel "whooa..God did that!" In New York City; where I live, on 9-11 some people got a miracle. People who decided to skip work or switch days off; or missed trains, or slept late, and it saved their lives.

I also know somebody, who had on her "Bucket List" to someday visit the Twin Towers. It meant so much to her she actually left a message in my voice mail the day before 9-11 to happily tell me she was finally getting to see it. She had an appointment there that morning, and died. Some people get the miracle, some people don't. Miracles, extraordinary experiences of being blessed by God's direct intervention in your life, can open up a heart; but not everybody gets them.

But there are three things that can open up a human heart that apply to all of us; and they may seem surprising.

1-Pure Joy
Have you ever laughed so hard your mouth, your face, your side, your stomach hurt? We all have that experience at some time in our life. Some live in that space more than others; but everyone gets a taste. Joy is the surest sign that God is hanging around, and it definitely opens up our hearts.

2-Being sorry for how you have screwed up.
And all of us have done that too. How does that work?

When I go to the juvenile jail every Friday afternoon there are several different things I do. Many times I talk with the residents about the *two sides of the rock* and *Jesus knocking*. Sometimes I do a violence prevention workshop, since many of the youth are in gangs. Sometimes I talk one-on-one with a resident, who requests it or the staff thinks could really use it.

I met with a fifteen year old I was told needed to talk to somebody. He comes in; and I see he's almost two or three times my size. He's huge- tall, built, arms bigger than my legs, tattoos everywhere, hardcore angry facial expression. I'm looking at him, and I'm thinking "this is going to be interesting". I'm also thinking that when they leave me alone with him, he could rip me to pieces in no time.

He sits down, and he starts crying. I can't believe I'm watching this big thug-like looking kid, who most people would run to the other side of the street if they saw him coming, crying his heart out.

He's crying because the day before, his mother had come to visit; and *she* couldn't stop crying. The last thing you ever think when you give birth to a child is that in the script of your life, you are ever going to some-day visit them in jail. He told me that from when he was little, he always knew how to find trouble; doing the wrong thing, getting in with the wrong people, lying, stealing, cheating. His mother had to watch him as he got older, committing more serious crimes, and getting more violent. Now he's got himself locked up behind bars in jail, and her heart is breaking. This young man is dying inside because he knows how much he is hurting his mother.

I don't know what he did. (I never ask.) He did tell me that he is in a gang. I know he was isolated at the jail; which is usually done for the protection of the other prisoners, because he could be violent. I know that most people would look at him and say: "you can't help him; he's a career criminal".

I know better. I watched how, with tears running down his face, without me saying anything, he begged Jesus to forgive him. He took his sorrow for how he hurt other people, he hurt himself and hurt his mother; and brought all of it to Jesus, and asked for His mercy and forgiveness. I watched him beg Jesus to help him be a better man.

Some of the youth I have met in jail are not sorry for anything. They have this chance to make a new beginning, and some don't want it. Some are even glad to be locked up; thinking that it will get them more respect when they get back on the street. Some refuse to give up their criminal ways, and have actually accepted that being locked up occasionally will always be a part of their lives. Some have said that when their mothers and grandmothers cry over them- well that's *their* problem.

This young man; I believe he's going to make it. I've seen it before; many kids in jail allowing their sorrow and remorse to become an open door to a new relationship with God; gaining from Him the strength to make a new beginning. Their hunger for God makes them open up to God's power and love; and through that they change.

Maybe you probably would never do the kinds of things that those in jail have done, or make the decisions that got them locked up; but really every single one of us has done things that were stupid, and selfish and ignorant; things that we're ashamed of. Those things don't jinx you with God. In fact they can open up the door to God by helping us realize our need for God in our lives; to admit that we're not so perfect, that we need help; that we need forgiveness and mercy and healing. All of us can relate to this.

What are the **big** things *you've* done wrong; that *really* messed up yourself or somebody else?

What are the things that you do a lot; that are not so serious, but know you shouldn't?

What are the good things that you *could* do, but never get around to?

Now ask Jesus for His forgiveness and commit yourself to changing, with His help.

If you are Catholic, consider receiving the powerful and healing Sacrament of Reconciliation; through which you can also receive the supernatural help to do better.

3-Healing for the painful things that life and other people have done to us.

Another thing that can really open up the heart; that applies to all of us, is the fact that people and life have hurt us. Every single one of us can relate to this; because we have all had a moment in our lives when we looked up at the sky and asked God: "Are you kidding me? You paying attention up there? You're looking after me? You love me? You care about me? You want what's best for me? Are you even real? Or are you just another fairy tale?"

There are people that believe that unless you've got some one little religious fact down you're not really in with God. Some people will say that unless you've visited a special spiritual place, you're not really there. It's actually very different. It's *everyday things* that bring you deepest into the heart of God:

Every single day of your life you will do something that hurts another person. Being sorry for that, and asking God's forgiveness can open up your heart.

Every single day of your life someone will do something to hurt you. Bringing that to God for healing can open up your heart.

Why am I sure this works?

I was a lost kid. I lived on the ugly side of the rock for 6 years: 7th grade thru 12th grade. I know what it feels like to be young; and not have Jesus in your life and not be flowing in the Holy Spirit. It's not that He wasn't knocking. I was closed. I not only didn't live in the fast lane; I didn't believe it was even there. Some people have one or two really extreme reasons why they slammed their door shut to God. That isn't my story. It was a lot of things added up.

I'm the oldest of nine kids. They say being the oldest child in any family is tough, because so much is expected of you. Also because parents are just learning how to be parents; you are the experiment. Most honest parents will admit they made their worst mistakes with their first one. I love my parents and I know they loved us and they did the very best they could; but when you are the oldest in a family of nine children, there is not much time for you; since obviously the most attention has to be given to the babies. The truth is; you become the third parent; and when they look at you all they can think of is what needs to be done. I'm not a selfish kid, I was glad to help; but after awhile you feel like a slave.

My father was hardly home. He is a factory worker, and he did not get paid fairly for the hard work he did. So he had to work a lot of hours to make up for the fact that he wasn't paid much per hour. He worked at one factory all day, ate his dinner, and worked at another factory at night. He worked at another factory on Saturdays; and often washed windows in apartment buildings on Sunday. Working for his family was his whole life. I knew he was doing it all for us, and I understood he had no time. I think all I would have liked was if he could have expressed that he wished it was different, that he wished we could have been closer.

My mother was also overwhelmed by raising all nine children by herself. Her whole focus was her family. The both of them did the very best they could, and I love them for that. There was also a lot of stress on them; and it was not easy for anyone.

In spite of all my fathers work and my mothers excellent management of whatever money we had; we struggled financially. We were the only family I knew that did not have a car. We wore other family's hand-me-downs. We often ate government cheese and peanut butter and oatmeal. We never took vacations; we hardly ever went anywhere. I worked hard delivering newspapers, shoveling snow and cutting grass; but much of the money helped pay the bills. I just didn't have what the other kids did. I felt God was blessing everyone else more than me. I'm not that great a student. I loved playing football, but was not built for it. I could never get the girls I liked to go out with me. My face broke out with acne. (*Not one or two zits; you could play connect the dots for hours on my face and never get bored*)

I know I'm **bringing you some Good News**; a message of hope. The knowledge that no matter where you have been, no matter what has happened to you; no matter what mistakes you have made, a life lived with and in God, a new life, a new beginning, the *Fast Lane* is waiting for you. If you are convinced there is no hope for you; let me tell you how truly lost I was: I sat alone in my High school cafeteria for four years. That's messed up. How did I go from being that kid, who didn't talk to anybody for four years, to someone who talks to hundreds and hundreds of groups of people a year, of all ages, that he never even met before; and with no notes?

I remember when it began to change. It was when I made a retreat at the end of high school. I remember some idiot was telling us "Jesus loves you" and all I just wanted to do was yell out "Shut up!". He continued over and over "Jesus loves you". I'm seething inside "You don't shut up mister, you're going to meet Jesus tonight!"

I even had a moment where I had it out with Jesus: "I am so sick of everyone telling me how much you love me. I never felt it. You blessed everybody better than me. But I have to do something. My attitude stinks, and I make everything worse than it needs to be. You know what; I'm interested. Hit me!"

I never got hit with a lightning bolt; but as I began to open up my heart and bring to Him all the hurts, all that garbage I had stored inside, I began to know His healing and loving power. God doesn't love me a tiny bit more than He loves you. You want to make a big difference in your life? Bring to Jesus what it was that hurt you. *Pain is not the only way to God; but it is the most definite.* The painful experiences in life that wound us; put us in a space where we are aware of our need, our dependence on our God.

Faith and trust in God are the foundation of life in the *Fast Lane.*

I did not make this up. We get it from Jesus Himself. He said very clearly that unless we become like little children, there is no place for us in heaven. He Himself called the Creator "Abba" which translates most perfectly as "daddy". When they asked Jesus how we should pray to our Creator, what does He go and say? "Our Father". He was clearly trying to teach us that as old and wise as we may become, in our hearts and souls and lives, we will always need our Creator the way a child needs their parent.

This message may not be attractive. Everyone wants to feel strong; that there is nothing the world is going to throw at us that we can't handle. In the United States, a society that has become used to defining itself by its power and success, people become addicted to having and maintaining power. All of us have watched people all our lives trying to be strong in stupid, ignorant ways:

* *acting* big and bad, bullying, intimidating, "Don't mess with me"

* *acting* like they don't care, killing off their emotional life, refusing to think, feel or talk about anything, believing that if they cut themselves off from negative emotions it will protect them

* *acting* like everything is a big joke, hoping to diminish the impact of negative emotions and experiences

* *acting* like they're superior to others, believing it will save them from negative contact

* *acting* like they're not even there, by being drunk, stoned, or medicated; thinking it's safer to stay out of the game of life all-together

Even though you have seen these behaviors around you all your life, and may have adopted one or more of these habits yourself; why am I inviting you to let them go? *One reason.*
They're not going to give you what you want.
They're not real. They're an *act.*
The only way to be **truly strong** is surprising:
It's to admit where you are weak; and then let God bless you right there with His healing and strengthening love and that's the real deal. What would that be for you?

What would you bring to God for healing?

There are countless things and many of them you may have been powerless to do anything about: **Loss**
Death
-Missing out on someone you never got to know at all that everyone else still talks about and you feel cheated.
-Getting the message out of nowhere that someone you love died in their sleep, an accident, or in a violent way and you didn't get to say goodbye, or tell them you loved them one last time. "It's not supposed to end like this"
-Praying that someone you love would get better and they didn't. Maybe you haven't prayed since they died; believing your prayers were wasted, and God won't listen to you.
-Suicide- A friend or family member takes their life, and you are devastated that you didn't see it coming or that your love wasn't enough reason for them to stay alive.
-Your mother losing a baby before or after you.

Divorce

It's often the beginning of a downward spiral. Many admit they started screwing up their life with their parents fighting and divorce. "They didn't care; I don't care"

-Living in a war zone. Living in a beautiful home and no one is happy in it. Seeing that the people who are supposed to be taking care of you; all they ever want to do is hurt each other. When adults are out of control it is unbearably frightening for a child.

-Blaming yourself. It's never the child's fault when parents split; but young children relate to everything personally and emotionally. "I was supposed to make them happy." Some are actually told they are the reason for their parents unhappiness.

-Being put in the middle of the conflict "Tell your mother this". "Don't tell your father that."

-Losing a parent. One goes on to make another family; and that becomes the focus of their life, and treats you like you're part of a huge mistake they made.

-Being mistreated by a parents' new spouse, boyfriend or girlfriend. Worse than that; your parent won't listen to you or takes their side instead of yours.

-parents who do not split; but do nothing but fight

Other Parents issues-

-Neglect- parents that buy you everything; but are not there for you. Living in a house that is more like a hotel than a home.

-Irresponsible parents- they will never be able to show you what is right because they don't do it themselves

-Cheating parent- one parent being unfaithful to the other and you are shocked and disappointed that they didn't know better.

-Rejection- Being told by your mother "I never should have had you". Being told you were an accident or mistake.

-Not having your Father's love.

Girls- wanting to be daddy's little girl- and for whatever reason you didn't get that: whether he wasn't there at all, or he didn't know how to relate to a daughter

Boys -wanting their father's love, pride, approval and attention and having a father unable to express those things, for whatever reason.

-Lies- Being lied to by a parent, even if it was done to protect you. Wondering how many other things are being kept from you. (Not talking about Santa!)

-Deceit & denial- Seeing something you weren't supposed to see, and being told "you didn't see that".

Addiction-
Alcohol-

-A parent or someone in your family who never knows when to stop, when enough is enough, and ruins every family party, sporting event or holiday.

-Being frightened someone you love is drinking and driving, and they may get killed and/or kill others.

-Memories of being stuck in a car where a parent drove drunk, and scared you were going to die

-Never inviting a friend to come over, sleep over, or even eat over; afraid your parent may have too much to drink, get sloppy, embarrass you and you might get known everywhere as the kid with the drunk parent.

-Having to watch a loved one's drinking get worse and worse over time, and worrying about how bad it might get

-Family get-togethers where everyone drinks too much and do and say things they shouldn't, and spend the rest of the year fighting about it

Drug abuse & addiction- legal & illegal

-A parent who does illegal drugs, and having to realize they will never be able to guide you the right way in life, because they don't do it themselves.

-A parent taking painkillers or some other legal drug, and they are increasingly out of it, not caring about anything anymore.

-A sibling stealing your money or your things and selling them for drugs

-A cousin you thought you'd grow up with, and your family doesn't want you near them because they are dealing and/or taking drugs.

-Someone you love dying because of their drug use

Gambling- A parent who gambles & loses money on-line or makes numerous trips to casinos or racetracks. Watching your family fight and your future suffer from gambling losses.

Smoking- Watching your parent or beloved relative or sibling engage in a habit that you know will destroy them. Trying so hard to get someone to stop smoking and they didn't.

Favoritism-
-Knowing a parent favors another sibling over you.
-Being compared unfairly & unfavorably to other family members.
-Not being treated fairly by teachers or coaches.
-Not being allowed to make a team or given a fair amount of playing time.

Disease, Disability & Injury
-Cancer- watching a good person suffer with this illness, who did nothing to deserve it
-Other diseases like diabetes, or arthritis, watching loved ones tortured by every movement
-Heart attack or stroke- they lived; but they might have another one and you'll lose them
-Autism- A sibling or family member born with this disease. Enduring the strain it can put on a family. The sadness from realizing how their life will be affected.
-Alzheimer's- watching a grandparent lose their mind, forgetting who they are, who you are, what they just said, what special memories that were shared, but now forgotten
-Injury- No longer being able to do the things you once could, participate in the activities you once enjoyed
Disability- You or someone you love having to live with and suffer through mental or physical disabilities.

Depression & other mental issues
- A parent or family member who never smiles or laughs, no matter how much you try to please them. Someone who spends all day in bed. Someone is on medication that makes them not really present.

-A parent who will not speak at meals, at night withdraws into their newspaper, TV, or computer. Living with a sibling who is lost and miserable.

-Someone in the family; especially a parent, with mental issues, or is mentally unstable, and you're frightened about something terrible happening.

Anger & Rage
-Living with someone who is angry and frustrated about how their life has gone, who finds fault with everything, is never happy, always looking for someone to blame for their own misery, or is always ready to explode.

Financial problems
-Parents business failed or lost their job, or investments lost.
-Parents fighting over financial issues.

Conflict
- Fighting with a close or best friend
- An enemy who is constantly creating problems for you
-A sibling is always fighting with you or your parent(s) and has turned the home into a war zone, a living hell
-An extended family feud, and there are relatives you might never see again and you feel hopeless about there ever being peace in the world, when there is no peace in your own family.

Violence & Abuse

-Being exposed to a dangerous person or situation where you were threatened by violence or scared of being killed or seriously injured

-Enduring mental, physical, sexual, verbal or emotional abuse

-Accidents- they can feel like an attack. Knowing that with another inch, or another second it wouldn't have happened, and when it does, you feel God abandoned you.

Betrayal & Rejection

-Cheating- finding out that someone who made a commitment to you was unfaithful.

-Someone revealing your secrets

-Losing a best friend, boyfriend or girlfriend- someone dumping you that you had such a strong feeling towards, and always thought would be a part of your life.

-Rejection of an older brother or sister that you just wanted to like you, and all they ever want to do is use you as a punching bag or find fault with you.

Moving

-You or your friend or family member moved, and the relationship changed, or did not survive the distance.

Tragedy

-War- someone in danger in a war situation overseas or someone in the family back from the war injured in body and/or soul.

-Someone suffering through a natural disaster- tornado, flood, hurricane, earthquake, wildfire etc.

Cruelty, disrespect and Humiliation
-Being bullied, in person, in a crowd of your peers, or on the internet.
-Being humiliated by a teacher, coach or another adult in front of others.

Pain as a result of your own personal failures:
Failure in school- feeling that you are always letting everyone down
Failure in sports- choking in a big situation and everyone blames you for the team's loss.
Embarrassment- being in a situation when you were not in control or made a big mistake in judgment and the outcome was embarrassing or terrible for others.

The Cross

The main symbol of all Catholics and Christians has always been the cross. They say that crucifixion is the most brutal way of killing people that humans have ever devised. They did not kill Jesus- He gave His life. They are two different worlds. We say this because everyone one who lived back then and met Jesus admitted that He did miracles. His followers, the people who loved and followed Him, of course included His miracles in the Bible. They wanted to make sure that all of us who are

coming around so many years later would know that when Jesus walked the earth, He did miracles.

There were other people. They thought he was a nice guy; but he wasn't the Messiah they were looking for. They admitted he did miracles.

The kicker here is that Jesus' enemies; the people who hated His guts, admitted that He did miracles. Who hated Jesus more than the Jewish priests? They knew He was performing miracles, and the crowds were running to Him. They knew they didn't have any such abilities and so would eventually lose all their followers and their power; so they did what they did.

There are two things that we grow from more than anything else:
great love
and great pain.
In Jesus' sacrifice for us on the cross they are both united.

So if everyone admitted Jesus did miracles; couldn't He have done a miracle?

Make nails disappear?

Put soldiers to sleep?

One little miracle, and the whole crowd screaming "Crucify him!" would have changed their minds.

So if Jesus didn't have to die like that, *why did He?*

Because He didn't want to spend eternity without us, and so He gave His life to save us all from our sins. What does that mean?

Face the facts: **you and I are never going to be good enough for heaven.** Today we have so much knowledge about the universe. The Hubbell telescope and satellites racing out into space are sending back to us amazing pictures of the universe; and it is all very mind-boggling. You can be looking at a single photograph taken by the Hubbell telescope, and they describe how many billions of galaxies you are looking at. Billions of galaxies! We can't even fathom that.

And this is just what God created!

What do you think HE must be like?

Now do you really think for a second that with all our sinfulness, smallness, stupidity and selfishness, when you die you could really go to the Creator of ALL THAT and say: "Hey that heaven thing; hanging out with you, hook me up, lets go, I deserve it"?

Never.

You and I will never be able to deserve heaven. It's a gift, and like every beautiful and valuable thing in life, it only exists because of a sacrifice. Jesus' death on the cross frees us from the cost of our sinful ways.

Anyone who is spoiled, and given so many things with no effort on their part; needs to know: *nothing that truly matters happens unless someone makes a sacrifice.*

Nothing good exists without someone's willingness to put themselves aside to allow the miracle of love to come into being; including and especially YOU. You will never need any further proof of this truth than your own life. Ask your mother what it was like to have to carry you around for nine months, and more importantly give birth to you. Did she ever shove that in your face? She deserves to. Childbirth is the most unbearable pain humans endure. If you were to ask your mother if she would like to go back and do it again, she would probably say "no way!" But she would tell you it was worth it; because the sacrifice of her physical pain of childbirth made it possible for you to have an *earthly life*.

Jesus' sacrifice on the cross makes it possible for you to have an *eternal life*. He wanted you to never doubt His love. Nothing, NOTHING says "I love you" more than someone willing to give their life for you. The next time you're thinking about who you want to follow ask yourself if that person did or would do that for you.

Jesus also wanted you to know that whatever personal pain you have suffered you could bring it to Him and know that He would understand; because He knows a lot about pain.

It's not over till it's over
But the cross is not the end of the story. There was a Resurrection. He was raised from the dead by His Father. This is a big deal because it means that there is a victory over sin and death and suffering. Whatever it was that broke your heart, that hurt you; it does not alone determine who you are. Those things do not have the last word. ***This is the Good News:*** that there is always a new beginning; a New Life in God. This is the foundation of a life lived in the *Fast Lane*. It's what makes the difference between traveling recklessly, or with grace.

Right this moment you can claim that victory:

Lord Jesus I thank You for the courage to be willing to look at myself and my life, and realize that right alongside all the fun, excitement and accomplishments; there have been these painful things. Lord I don't want to get caught up in feeling bad about myself and my life, and have a little pity party. I want to bring it all to you; knowing that doing this is not going to make these things magically disappear.

Lord, you already know where I got hurt. I trust that if I give to you my weakest link; I will find in you my greatest strength. Take where my heart is broken, and put it back together the way you know it is meant to be.

(Bringing it all to Jesus, you are giving him permission to touch your heart and your life with His healing power where you have been hurt the most.)

Lord, the way it is for you; is the same way for me. It's worse, it's harder to watch someone you love suffer than to be hurt yourself. Right now I bring to you whoever there is in my life who is hurting, or lost, or screwing up their life.

(Ask Jesus to bless and be with them and through what they're going through.)

Lord Jesus I pray that I will always remember that I can bring my whole life to you; the joyful and the painful. Help me to always put You first, to depend on no one and nothing more than You and through it all, thank you for Your grace Your love, Your healing power in my life. Amen

What next?

So what do you do with the things you are bringing to Jesus for healing? This prayer holds the answer:

> **The Serenity Prayer**
> *God grant me the serenity*
> *to accept the things I cannot change;*
> *courage to change the things I can;*
> *and wisdom to know the difference.*

Some things that happen to us we can't do anything about; and our prayer is for the peace or serenity to accept them in our life:
*death *divorce   *accidents   *sickness & injury

Sometimes our prayer is for the courage to try to do something about what is painful in our life:
*making peace with a sibling, friend or enemy
*speaking to a parent, sibling, family member or friend about their drug or alcohol problem (try an intervention)
*parents fighting or bringing you into the middle of their disputes
*fighting with a friend or a friendship breaking up

How will God heal you?

If you are feeling "All this heavy stuff; now what do I do?"

Here is exactly what to do with your pain:

1- Bring it to Jesus.

You may be afraid that you have been through so much, that there is no way God can help you. Or you may feel "I know other people who have been through things way worse than me. My problems are so small compared to them. I shouldn't even bother Jesus."

There is no problem too big or too small for Jesus Christ. The only hurt that He can't heal is the one you don't tell Him about. It's not that you have to inform Jesus. He already knows exactly where and how you got hurt. This is about you opening the door to your heart, and giving Him permission to touch you with His healing power. Remember: *God doesn't give you anything to deal with the you and he cannot handle together.*

2- Bring it so someone you trust.

The key word here is trust. All of us at some time make the mistake of trusting someone, who proved to be untrustworthy and we got hurt; maybe even badly. Some people put everything out in the open, and learn the hard way that telling everybody everything is not a smart idea. Not everyone cares about your problems, and some people will even use your weakness against you some day. So when deciding who you will talk to; think and pray about who you should trust.

Who won't reject or humiliate you? Who has had some valuable life experience and will understand? Who is a godly person who will guide you on the right path?

If you honestly feel you have no one you can trust; contact me. I'm not a professional counselor; but I'll be happy to be there for you and I'll do whatever I can. I don't want anyone to be alone with what they're going through.

3- *Offer it up.*

Lifting up your suffering for the good of someone or something else has tremendous impact on the spiritual level; making an impact on the lives of others here and in the larger reality. Our sacrifices can help change things, and heal souls in this world and the next.

4- *Bring it to a Counselor.*

Counseling can be one of the ways in which God heals. If your reaction is "NO- I tried counseling. the idiot sat there for 40 minutes and just nodded and took the money". That can happen. It's like anything else; there is good and there is bad. If you had a bad experience; don't give up on counseling; try somebody else.

Notes on counseling:

1- Some in the psychotherapy field are not into helping people figure things out; and just want to prescribe medication. If you walk in to a psychiatrists office and they don't even listen to you, and just start writing out a prescription for an anti-depressant, or they ask you what medication you would like?- GET OUT.

2- If you should need a medication as a short-term aid; make sure you get solid advice about how to know when you can start cutting down the doses, and maybe even eventually eliminate it. Make sure the doctor knows that your goal is if possible to live a medication-free life. You may have to be strong about this.

Some people need medication to function. That's not what I'm talking about. Many in the medical and psy-

chiatric professions today have become legal drug push-
ers, and are not serving God's will.

3- Some problems like eating disorders, cutting, rape, and
sexual abuse require a special knowledge to help a person work through what has happened to them. Check in
advance if the counselor you are going to has this knowledge. For example: the person cutting themselves needs
specific help in re-wiring their brain to stop that behavior.
If your counselor says "Oh, you just have poor self es-
teem"- GET OUT

4-Never, never go for counseling alone. Bring Jesus with
you. Many in the field do not have a Catholic, Christian
or even spiritual perspective- so it's up to you to make
sure Jesus is working through the session with you by
consciously inviting Him in and praying with Him after.

What *not* to do with your pain:

1-Don't Ignore it- things don't go away, they only eventually raise their ugly heads later on at the worst possible
time, and in the worst possible way. Deal with your emotions of anger, fear and pain. You may have been through
something that you are angry about. Many times underneath anger is fear and pain. You may even angry at God.
Think about it; you have probably gotten angry at some
point with almost everyone you have ever loved. Keep it
real with God, who wants to know exactly how you feel.
So if you feel "God, sometimes I don't like the way you
run your universe" get it out, but remember to also say
"but I do love You and trust You and want to believe in
You and follow You, so please help me." Many times

people do not know how to release anger without cutting the person off. Questioning, getting frustrated with God is *not* a problem; holding onto anger, cursing and blaming Him and slamming the door to your heart in His face *is*.

2- *Don't medicate with drugs or alcohol*.

How often you have seen in movies, and TV, and maybe even in your own family, when someone gets really bad news, they pour themselves a drink or pop a pill. We live in a society that pushes drugs for every possible thing (often with ridiculous lists of side effects) and sends the message consciously and subconsciously that you should *never* feel any pain. Pain is a part of life; be willing to go through it. If after awhile you are still stuck, get help.

> **A word about drugs & alcohol:**
> We now know more than ever about the dangers associated with these substances; yet young people and adults continue to drink and drug in record numbers and amounts. Drugs and alcohol give you the illusion of the shiny side of the rock. The key word is illusion. The buzz you get is the feelings of the brain cells dying. (Be careful- you may be like me: with not that many brains cells in the first place and can't afford to lose too many!) That good feeling you get from a substance; you were meant to have naturally. It comes when you have the Holy Spirit inside you. It's *not* that your life becomes a party. It's *not* that you should become addicted to feeling good. It's that you carry within you the sense that being you is a good thing, and living your life with all it's challenges, is a gift. It is a blessing to be alive. D*on't stop until you have that without a substance.*

Part 2

The most important part of life is relationship. We can live without a lot of things; but we cannot live without love. Life is a love affair. Living in the *Fast Lane* is **not easy;** *but it is simple.* **It is about Jesus, and our relationship with Him.**

The first part:
We let Jesus love us; accepting and receiving Him
The second part: we follow Jesus by loving Him back
by loving each other.

I have this statue in front of my home in Queens Village, New York City. Every once in awhile, someone will knock at my door trying to be helpful, (usually it's a little old lady) informing me "someone stole the hands off your statue."

I have to explain to them that I mean for the statue to be this way; to show the way it really is; that in this world today, Jesus has no hands.

He once did. He had a whole body, and He gave His life on the cross for us. Jesus wants to bring His love into this physical reality now, and help us all become who the Creator made us to be. He works through those of us who have given ourselves to Him. We are His hands!

> *Christ has no body but yours,*
> *No hands, no feet on earth but yours,*
> *Yours are the eyes with which he looks Compassion on this world,*
> *Yours are the feet with which he walks to do good,*
> *Yours are the hands, with which he blesses all the world.*
> *Yours are the hands, yours are the feet,*
> *Yours are the eyes, you are his body.*
> *Christ has no body now but yours,*
> *No hands, no feet on earth but yours,*
> *Christ has no body now on earth but yours.* -St Teresa

What are YOU doing here?

What have you been told is important in this life?

To be popular? Then people will like you and you will connect well with people..

To be intelligent? Then you will likely have a good job.

To be athletic? Then you will be able to compete and demonstrate your prowess.

There is nothing wrong with being popular, intelligent and athletic.

But: have you been to Sea World?

The dolphins are very sociable, very smart, and very agile. You obviously were not born to be a dolphin.

While there have been some examples of animals exhibiting altruistic behavior; what makes human beings unique among all of God's creation is the capacity to consistently give and receive love. This is who you are. This is what you were born for. Everything God creates, is created for a purpose. The purpose of human beings and human life is the giving and receiving of love. Look into your own heart. Remember the moments that have truly meant the most in your life. You'll discover you already KNOW this to be true.

If you ever think the Catholic or Christian faith, that being a friend and follower of Jesus is boring; *you didn't get it.* Why am I sure of that? I've looked for adventure. I've been skydiving. I've jumped out of planes thousands of feet in the air. I've been bungee jumping. I've been off-Broadway, movies, TV shows, commercials. I've been the first white man in some remote villages in Africa. I was in the crossfire when a major revolt sprung up in a small Asian country.

I have found all of these things are nothing compared to the adventure of being best friends with Jesus; of being someone who can spend their whole day with Him, sharing with Him in his adventures of loving. If you find something better than this, let me know. I'll change religions tomorrow.

When Jesus knocks at your door; He doesn't just say "Hey kid, have a nice day!" He invites you to come out and play. He's asking you to join Him in the adventure of loving; of making this world into an expression of the heaven we are hopefully going home to.

If you open your heart to Jesus; if you give Him your hands; He will give you his eyes. He will show you what He sees. He will show you the person:

-whose grandparent has just been rushed to the hospital
-wearing a sad face, who is an outcast in your school or
    even in their own family
-whose dog just died
-who has been told in so many ways that they are worth-
    less and has begun to believe it
-who has given up on love and intimacy because of being
    sexually used or abused
-who can't take one more beating or betrayal
-who is scared to death their mother might die of cancer
-who wants to kill their alcoholic father.
-who feels like a failure
-who blames themselves for everything

The list of secret pains of those around you is endless. Every single person has a story. Every single person is looking for love, respect and acceptance; and God is giving you the opportunities and abilities to save lives.

There is so much to be done. We need you. We don't live right on this earth. There is not enough love in the world; not even close. We are so far away from the way the Creator intends for us to live that it's ridiculous. Opportunities to love are everywhere; just look around. Remember: every school shooting you will ever hear about; every suicide you will ever know of; is some person who, maybe at the right moment if someone would have been kind to them, and been the presence of Christ to them, maybe it wouldn't have happened.

So much of what we call human history is tribal warfare; one group getting what they want by taking it away from another. So much of what we call human relationships is manipulating others for advantage and personal benefit. All of it: brutal middle lane living.

But God did not give up on the human race. He's here, and He's got you here. You're in the world at a key time in human history. Life cannot continue down this path down this spiraling vortex of self-absorption, greed and hate much longer. Your generation is here to save the human race. But if you don't do the good things that you can do now; you'll never get to the big stuff later. The important news is that the little things are not little. Every loving act, no matter how small or unrecognized affects the physical and spiritual reality. Go out there and rock the planet.

You are invited by Our Savior to be the change you want to see in the world.

Who can you love right now? Everyone is your brother and sister. I've had the chance to pray with Navajo Native Americans in their sweat lodges. and seen their deep sense of connection to their extended clan. During the experience there is a beautiful tradition of remembering all those they are connected to by saying:

"All my relations!"

Always, by loving the others we are loving Jesus through them.

*In Christ we're **all** related:*

* parents
* siblings
* grandparents
* family relatives
* little ones
* friends
* enemies
* neighbors
* strangers
* classmates, fellow employees
* the poor and those who suffer
* the lost, lonely, sad, outcast, forgotten

There are so many you can give love to, if you only have eyes to see. Driving, living in the *Fast Lane* means you love who might be right in your midst who wants and needs the love of God. Never doubt that His love is enough.

Love is the only thing in this world that the more you give it away, the *more* you have to give, not less.

In one of the apparitions of Jesus' Mother Mary, she appeared with beams of light radiating out of her hands. When asked what they were; Mary responded "These are the graces that nobody even thinks to ask for".

(Grace is the word used for the power and love of God.)

Let yourself feel how huge that is. It means that we all live in a universe where there is more love here than we can even imagine, or think to ask for.

We are given the blessing and privilege to be someone through whom God can bless the world. He can pour out those graces through us and our simple humble lives.

That's why we say ***"God is good all the time"***.

Section 2
Challenges of the Road

Roadblocks & potholes

GPS & Accidents waiting to happen

So if you've decided to live life as much as you can in the *Fast Lane*, and give your soul, and your life to God, things will never be the same. *It will not be easy.* There are countless things within and around you to make it difficult to navigate this road. In this section we will cover dealing with those dangers and challenges.

Danger ahead

No matter where you live; traveling is not easy, and can actually at times be very dangerous. In developed countries roads may be well-paved but the danger is often the large number of cars on the highways, and that they are moving very quickly. In places like South America, Asia and Africa, the danger can come from the road not being well constructed. I have been in dangerous situations where rain had made traveling dirt roads difficult if not impossible.

Road Signs

Road signs exist to alert you to possible danger, and guide you to travel & arrive safely. To be spiritually alive in the Holy Spirit is to be able to remain alert, reading the signs everywhere that you are on the right track, or may be headed for trouble.

The world, the flesh, and the devil

In winter driving there can be a very dangerous situation known as "black ice". This happens when there is frozen water on the road, and you can't tell because the black pavement looks normal. Some people slip and fall, and become seriously injured. Cars can pile up in horrible highway collisions. Black ice is just like the way temptations and unresolved emotions, if not heeded, can cause terrible accidents and damage.

Again, life is not easy; and you should not expect that the *spiritual* life will be anything less than the most challenging adventure you will ever set out on.
It's been said that this earthly life is a constant battle with: the world, the flesh, and the devil.

1-the world- since the first humans turned away from God, the paradise God intended this earth to be has been corrupted by sin, and is getting worse constantly. We are all constantly surrounded by people making selfish, sinful, ignorant choices. Allowing those people to guide your decisions, and wanting to fit in with them, can be a danger to your soul.

2-the flesh- we have to remember our own personal tendency to sin, to reject God, and live life consumed with our own personal pleasure and security instead of loving. This includes issues of sexual temptation; but is not limited to it.
Sexual desire is something that God gave humans, and actually all animals. There is no continuation of life without it. The thing that makes sexual activity different for

humans is that we are not just animals. We are not here to merely exist. All human activity, especially intimate physical interaction is for the purpose of expressing love.

Our sexuality is a gift. It was created for us, and to be used by us *for life-* the *life* of a marriage and to bring *new life* into the world. All human activity is for the expression of love; the transcendence of self. Our sexuality is the most complete gift of ourself to another; but urges of the flesh can be a great source of temptation.
Your body will never stop crying out for your attention- for food, rest and every possible gratification.

3- the devil- There are spiritual beings who have rejected God. They do not serve the Creator, and they do not want us to either. These evil beings are allowed to exist in this reality, and they strive to steal as many souls away from God as possible. Learning how to be on your guard and reject their temptations, allows humans to grow spiritually stronger.

Some people don't believe in the devil. They believe it's an old fairy-tale, a superstition, or a symbolic depiction of the existence of evil. But the devil *is* real, and perhaps his greatest weapon is to try and convince you he doesn't exist. *Saying you don't believe in him is not going to protect you from him.* Never seek power at any cost (That's what the fallen angels did.) It opens the door to evil.
There is no need to get paranoid. Remember Satan and his power are not equal to Jesus.

Temptation & Sin
Avoid temptation at all cost. With every temptation, someone is there ready to take advantage. There is a difference between sin and temptation. Even Jesus was tempted. Sin is consciously choosing to turn away from God.

These are considered the seven deadly sins:

ENVY	SLOTH	GLUTTONY	
WRATH	PRIDE	LUST	GREED

These choices lead away from God and often to disaster, and make *Fast Lane* travel impossible.

Addiction
It is extremely difficult, and may even be impossible to have a true spiritual life while in the grip of an addiction. They block the flow of God's love in our lives.

How to tell if you're addicted?

If you do not feel fully alive unless you are engaged in a particular behavior or taking a specific substance, you're addicted. It's not only that the behavior that consumes you; it's also the constant thinking about it, and an inability to resist the cues that set you up for it as well.

> If addiction runs in your family; for example if alcoholism has ruined family members, you've got to be careful. When it comes to alcohol; some people can take it or leave it. Some people will respond to it in an addictive way. There is scientific proof that tendencies run genetically in families. If the men in your family have had issues with alcohol, even if they are recovered; and you are a guy- the chances are 90% you have inherited the tendency.

When you have an addiction, it is like the engine and transmission of your vehicle have been severely damaged. You may be barely able to continue on your journey with a compromised vehicle, but you endanger every one around you and eventually you will break down, maybe even in a horrible way.

Addictions & Compulsive behaviors can include:

Alcohol	Bodybuilding/ Steroids
Co-dependency	Drugs (legal & illegal)
Eating disorders	Gambling
Hoarding	Nicotine
Pornography	Self Mutilation
Sex	Shoplifting
Shopping	Video games
Work	Caffeine
Social networking	

Anger, fear & pain

Street Soldiers have been very successful in helping young people leave behind the negative life of the street and rebuild their lives. I've been trained by them, and I am very proud to be a Street Soldier. They teach a treatment plan for the disease of violence; which includes removing from your life the things that can lead to a violent lifestyle. There are risk factors that make it likely you will have violence in your life. They've been motivating and helping the young people to eliminate these risk factors for years; but found it was not enough. There are also underlying emotional issues that if not dealt with, rise up and knock down the person's progress. So they integrated into their treatment plan the necessity of dealing with the underlying emotions of: anger, fear and pain.

Anger

It is helpful, even crucial for you to explore what is it that you are angry about. When there is something from your past that you never dealt with and released; it comes out in other ways that end up causing problems in your life. One of the ways I try to explain how this works with the young people I work with in jail is: think back on a time when you got up in the middle of the night to pee. It was dark; you couldn't see where you were going, and you stubbed your toe or banged your foot. The next day your toe hurts every time it touches something. It wasn't all those things that rubbed against your foot during the day that were the problem; it was the fact that you had been injured.

It's also like if you have ever had a toothache; and then everything you put in your mouth after that- hot, cold, sweet, sour bothers you. It's not all those food and drinks that created the problem; it's that the tooth was sensitive.

It's the same with anger. When not dealt with, it affects and infects everything. Who are you angry with: God? someone else? yourself?

Fear

The brain functions like a computer. It's job is to protect you. To achieve that, the brain will never stop trying to prevent you from ever undertaking anything that might lead to difficulty, danger or pain. It does this by trying to make you afraid of that activity or situation.

Just as any computer has to be plugged in, turned on, and operated by a person in order to do anything; remember it is *you* who runs the computer of your brain. The person who is living in the *Fast Lane* dedicates their brain to be guided by the Holy Spirit. Having a spiritual life, committed to God is the only way to be vigilant, without being paranoid. (Obviously sometimes it is useful, even necessary for survival to listen to the brain. The voice that says "don't step in front of that oncoming truck unless you want to be squashed like a pancake" should always be listened to.)

How do you know when to listen to, and when to ignore the brain and the fears it promotes? **Prayer, God's Word, your religion, seeking the input of godly spiritual mentors, and constantly consciously asking God for guidance.**
There is no need to waste huge amounts of energy fighting fear. When it is not helpful, just simply say "thank you very much for warning me; but I have to do this anyway."

Pain

Pain is a part of human life. No one goes through life without some form of mental, physical, emotional, or relational pain. Even Jesus; God's Son, did not get to go through an earthly existence without pain. He cried when people He loved died. He endured the personal physical torture, the horror and humiliation of scourging and crucifixion. When we do not deal with pain by going through it; it can lead to many unhealthy things like violence against self, others or both.

Disrespect for life

It is essential to respect the potential that is inherent in all forms of life; and most especially human life, from conception to grave. You don't take a human life, even and especially defenseless human life. One quarter of all pregnancies worldwide end in abortion. This is a slap in the face to the Creator. You simply don't do to another what you would not want to be done to you. No one in their right mind wishes their mother had killed them. There are many "Life issues". There is more and more widespread cruelty and disrespect for life in the world: demonizing others, endless war, terrorist acts, pollution and the devastation of the earth, economic injustice, bullying, slavery, human trafficking to name a few.

Guilt

Guilt is a **good** thing. It is your soul letting you know you have gone against your conscience; against what you know is right in your creator's eyes. *Guilt trips* are **not** a good thing; played out by manipulative people; or something a person does to punish their own self.

We are all capable of being idiots, and all our smallness, selfishness, sinfulness and stupidity affects the whole. If you cannot admit your guilt, you can have no integrity. If you cannot let God forgive you, you will feel hopeless and live chaotically; figuring that you are already screwed, so you might as well just keep it going.

We are immersed in an ocean of God's mercy. It is true on one level; that what goes around comes around; but in Christ we are freed of the cycles of karma, and as His followers we do not live in fear of our mistakes coming back to haunt or jinx us. In Christ there is always the possibility of a new beginning.

> **"it's a minor set-back for major comeback."**
> a young man I met @ the juvenile jail

Isolation

Seung-Hui Cho was the young man who committed the Virginia Tech massacre, the deadliest shooting incident by a single gunman in American history. "Shine" was his favorite song, and these lyrics were written on the wall of his dorm room.

> *Teach me how to speak*
> *Teach me how to share*
> *Teach me where to go*
> *Tell me love will be there.*
> **Shine** Collective Soul

Before his terrible tragic act of killing 32 people and wounding 25 others that day; he wrote: "you had a hundred billion chances and ways to have avoided today. You forced me into a corner and gave me only one option. Now you have blood on your hands that will never wash off."

He obviously had serious problems; yet there was still a part of him that hoped for a life of human connection. These are times of increased soul-killing isolation. God has wired us to be in relationship, and to be connected to each other and without connection life is unbearable.

Three different 13 year old girls from three different churches and schools, but all in the same county in upstate New York had taken their lives within a six month period. They had each been on a Confirmation retreat with me within months of taking their lives. I heard of the third death when I was doing retreats at the high school they all would have been attending the following school year. My heart was heavy, and I begged the students for help. "They were with me. I gave them the Good News. I thought I gave them a reason for hope. I thought I laid out for them a way to go through life no matter what it might throw at them. What did I miss? What am I not saying clearly enough? Please help me. God has me going out to reach your generation for Him. What do I need to know about young people today so I can help save more lives?"

No sooner did I finish asking the question, when a student's hand went up, and she said "we're lonely." My first reaction was "are you kidding me? How can that possibly be? Your generation more than any other is in constant contact with each other: Facebook, emails, texting, cell phones, tweeting. What do you mean, "we're lonely?"". She replied "those things don't mean anything". To this day no young person has ever disputed that.

We are constantly in contact, yet it is often on a superficial level and many feel isolated.

If you are reading this and:

- you are a loner?

-or you are so angry for the way you have been treated that you want so badly to hurt someone?

-or do you feel no one understands and you would never hurt anyone else; but you don't want to be here anymore? ***Please get help.*** Please let someone you trust know how bad you are hurting.

Boredom

I sometimes hear young people say that they're bored. I just can't relate to that. It probably means they don't have a sense of what an amazing gift that life is. There is just so much creating, learning, exploring, and loving to do in this life. There is a saying most actors become familiar with: "there are no boring parts; there are only boring actors".

Judging

Every time I have ever judged; I have stepped out of God's light. Judging blocks us from loving, and for that reason alone, it is deadly. Your brain will never stop giving you reasons why you should refuse to love someone. (Remember: its job is

> *If we are busy judging people, we have no time to love them.*
> **Mother Teresa**

to protect you.) With God's grace, you can resist the temptation to look at someone and see only their sins. Each person *is* imperfect, *and* is deeply loved by the Creator. Everyone you will ever meet is looking for kindness, compassion, generosity, forgiveness, acceptance, freedom, and love. God will test you to see if you will be faithful to that one person who is a challenge; and you will not be able to go forward with Him until you are.

One time as soon as I walked in to lead a retreat; I was told by the person in charge; "there is a boy in the front row and he is going to try and ruin your retreat". Apparently he had tortured several different Confirmation teachers, and was always in trouble, and they were sure was going to wreck the retreat as well.

Yet as the retreat went on , not only did he *not* ruin it, he made the most of it. He laughed out loud at all the funny moments. He led the others by example; by being the first one to keep it real during the sharing session. If I would have judged him based on the experiences of others, I would have ruined the day, for him, for me, and everyone else there. He even turned me on to a scene at the end of the movie *Stranger than Fiction* that I have used many times on retreats. It's a scene about what a blessing life is, and how God uses the little things in our lives to strengthen and nurture us.

He was a gift to me that day. A gift that, had I judged, I would have missed. This is only one story of so many times where I'm learning that appearances, and past experiences are *not* more powerful than what the Holy Spirit can do in any given moment. The minute I judge, I step out of the here and now where God is creating something new. When I judge, I can no longer be His instrument, and I can no longer be blest by the gift offered to me. When I judge I deny the reality, that in each new moment; in God's Spirit there is always the chance to make a new decision, and create a new momentum, and create a new reality.

> *As Harold took a bite of Bavarian sugar cookie, he finally felt as if everything was going to be ok. Sometimes, when we lose ourselves in fear and despair, in routine and constancy, in hopelessness and tragedy, we can thank God for Bavarian sugar cookies. And, fortunately, when there aren't any cookies, we can still find reassurance in a familiar hand on our skin, or a kind and loving gesture, or subtle encouragement, or a loving embrace, or an offer of comfort, not to mention hospital gurneys and nose plugs, an uneaten Danish, soft-spoken secrets, and Fender Stratocasters, and maybe the occasional piece of fiction. And we must remember that all these things, the nuances, the anomalies, the subtleties, which we assume only accessorize our days, are effective for a much larger and nobler cause. They are here to save our lives. I know the idea seems strange, but I also know that it just so happens to be true.*   Stranger than Fiction

Laziness & Procrastination

When you have everything handed to you it can be difficult to push yourself. Most young people admit to being lazy. Many people of all ages are also procrastinators; putting everything off the difficult or unpleasant tasks to the last minute. You don't want to learn the hard way.

My grandmother on my father's side, my Nani, lived in Bridgeport Connecticut, where I was born. We moved to Long Island when I was six, and didn't visit much after that. Practically every time we did see her, she would always say to me the same thing; "that I should go into show business, and sing, dance, and tell jokes, and make a lot of money". I was a shy quiet kid who didn't talk to the kid next to me; never mind get up and entertain in front of people. She never relented, and I never stopped thinking she had the wrong guy.

I got the word she was very sick and hospitalized; and I wanted to go and visit. I was working three jobs that summer, and trying to coordinate a day off from all three so I could make the trip up there & back. Then I heard that she was doing better, so I thought I'd just put off visiting until my schedule would be easier to manage. In spite of doing so much better, she took a nap and never woke up.

At the funeral home, as I looked at her in the casket, it hit me: *my whole life is up in front of people.* Maybe I'm not singing and dancing; but every day, all day I'm up in front of people. She had seen that in me; long before I could see it in myself. I was standing over her body, realizing what a gift she was in my life; when my aunt, who lived up there came over to me and says "you know, she asked to see you everyday." I don't wish on anybody hearing those words or the horrible feeling it brought up in me. I felt so sick inside I literally threw up. I was so upset, I stayed outside the funeral home for two days. Everyone was coming out after me; "what's *wrong* with you?" One of the hardest things I ever had to do was to help carry her casket in and out of the church for the funeral mass. I wanted to do that so much out of respect; but the whole time, all I could feel was, "what's the point now; this body in this coffin is not her. When she was in this body; I wasn't there for her."

I understand that she knew, and knows now how I feel toward her; but I also know she would have loved to have seen me one more time.

I was the first grandson. I was her favorite. I never got to say "I love you. Thanks for believing in me and encouraging me. I'll see you in heaven."

I had done with my Nani what I did with a lot of things in my life in those days; putting off the good I could do; thinking I had all the time in the world. I had the idea to go visit her. I just made excuses to push it off till later. Now, I don't walk around scared everyone in my life is going to die at any moment; but if I get an idea, if I have a chance to do something good, I do it. I hope you learn from my mistake. There are people very close to you who want and need your love. You don't want to be cheap or lazy. We just don't know how long we will have each other in this life.

Jealousy

Jealousy of the talents, success and good fortune of others comes from a deprivation mentality, which will always diminish your life. Jealousy is connected to the belief that there is not enough to go around, and so if others have so much, it means there will not be enough for me. It is incompatible with travel in the *Fast Lane.* Decide: will you live in *faith* in God's abundance or *fear* of deprivation?

Another form of jealousy comes from measuring yourself against others. To compare yourself, and be jealous of the talents, status, or possessions of another is foolish; because you were not born to to be them. You were born to be the best you; so accept and love your life!

Pride

Pride is arrogant puffing yourself up, and there is no place for it in a life in the *Fast Lane*. It is different from self-esteem and self-respect.

> **Vanity, definitely my favorite sin.**
> - Devil in Devils Advocate

Selfishness

Devil's Advocate is a movie where Al Pacino plays the devil. In this movie he lays out the trap of selfishness to steal every soul away from God:

"You sharpen the human appetite to the point where it can split atoms with its desire; you build egos the size of cathedrals; fiber-optically connect the world to every eager impulse; grease even the dullest dreams with these dollar-green, gold-plated fantasies, until every human becomes an aspiring emperor, becomes his own God... and where can you go from there? And as we're scrambling from one deal to the next, who's got his eye on the planet? As the air thickens, the water sours, and even the bees honey takes on the metallic taste of radioactivity. And it just keeps coming, faster and faster. There's no chance to think, to prepare. It's buy futures, sell futures, when there is no future! We got a run-away train boy, we got a billion selfish Bozos all jogging into the future. Every one of 'em getting ready to steal from God's ex-planet, lick their fingers clean. And then it hits home! You gotta pay your own way. It's a little late in the game to buy out now! Your belly's too full, your eyes are bloodshot, and you're screaming for someone to help! But guess what? There's no one there! You're all alone. You're God's special little creature.

Free will! I don't make you do anything. I lay the temptations out there. I make them look real good, and you suckers are lapping it all up!
                        the Devil in "Devil's Advocate"

Selfishness is a disease that kills souls. It is the founda-tion of life in the middle lane, and stuck in it, makes traveling the *Fast Lane* impossible. You may be able to resist many other temptations; but the final trap that has been set to steal your soul away from God is to get you to wrap your whole life around you. If all you ever think about when you make your life's decisions is: "what about me? What's going to be easiest for me. What's in this for me? What's going to make me feel good? Look good? What's going to give me the greatest comfort, advantage, benefit, convenience? What about me?" Then the devil got you!

People have always been selfish; it's back in the Bible. Jesus had a whole lot to say about it. But never have people been as selfish as they are today. We have all been programmed by our society, and some even been spoiled by their own family to be narcissistic; to be the center of their universe and live a lifestyle of self gratification, self pleasure, self indulgence, self abandonment, and self-worship.
Your life will always be a struggle between:

<u>Fast Lane</u>	*versus*	<u>middle lane</u>
<u>culture of Christ</u>	*versus*	<u>the culture of the world</u>
What's good for love		what feels good for me
What's good for growth		what's good for pleasure
What is for the people		what is good for profit

Never before has the trap been set more completely. You are surrounded by so much of it that you could easily succumb to believing that it is the way you should live: "This how you do it- you take care of yourself and don't worry about anyone else." You could get the impression that Jesus' Gospel of loving is a fairy tale that they preach; but nobody actually lives.

Remember: selfishness and greed eventually destroy every person and community that practice them.

Despair

Depression sets in when we feel immobilized. The problems of life, and this world can feel overwhelming. Do not cave in to despair. Be patient; most growth is gradual. How do you climb Mt. Everest? Gradually, not straight up. You progress, step back, camp, get acclimated, and then progress some more. Repeat as needed. *Same way with life!*

We live in a time of instant results and deep down we have come to believe everything should happen quickly and easily. When it doesn't; despair can kick in; and that is a sure sign you have forgotten to trust and put what is concerning you into God's hands. In Ghana, Africa I found that people there have a deep patience and acceptance. Many people paint their favorite religious sayings on their vehicles, and so many buses and trucks say "God's time".

There is another saying "God may not come when you call; but He's always on time!". In a fast-moving culture it can be easy to forget these basic truths.

Peer Pressure

So many people these days have not given themselves to God. Many have been raised to focus on the middle lane, and have decided that the *Fast Lane* does not exist or that it is not worth traveling. Some attempt to humiliate those who do give their lives to God. Following the crowd will usually not lead to anything good. We are called to be *in* the world, but not *of* it.

Section 3

Navigating the Road- The Art of Driving

Road Signs & Repairs

GPS   First things first.   *Have you found Jesus?*

I get asked this a lot when I travel or meet Christians who may not be Catholic (I'm amazed how often they are often pretty sure our religion is not really about Jesus.) Anyway I usually use these moments to flex my sarcastic sense of humor.

"Have you found Jesus?" *Gee, I didn't know he was missing.*
"Have you found Jesus?"

   Oh, I'm sorry, was it my job to look for him? Nobody told me.
"Have you found Jesus?"

              Oh Yes, he was behind the couch the whole time.

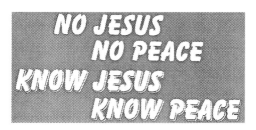

The foundation of the *Fast Lane* is Jesus; allowing Him to be your Savior and best friend, and inviting the Holy Spirit to live in you. From that flows a new life; life lived in the *Fast Lane*.

The Bible- the owners manual

Don't try to follow Jesus without reading the instructions. Make it a habit to read at least a few lines from the Bible every day. Some people like to start at the beginning "Genesis " and go from there. Some like to open the Bible up randomly, close their eyes, point to a line, and then read what they've selected. I personally recommend starting with the New Testament; especially the four Gospels; where Jesus is actually walking and talking. A good place to follow up after that are the Letters, which have lots of important insights and tips for everyday life.

The Code

*How we are supposed to travel this road of life?*In the film "the Road" which talks place in a post-apocalyptic world; a father and son are struggling to survive. The father knows he doesn't

> before you do anything always **ask: WWJD?** (what would Jesus do?

have long to live, and he's trying to make sure he teaches his little boy what he absolutely has to know: *"We don't eat people and we carry the light within"*. It pretty much summarizes our code as people who love and follow Jesus. In the movie, it means literally not eating people. For us it means that we do not use and devour others for our own benefit. We carry the light within, and we live by the guidance of the Holy Spirit regardless of what anyone else around us is doing.

It gets ugly when people don't know how to live. I was riding in a New York City subway train, and an obviously disturbed woman spit in the face of a middle-aged businessman. People are egging him on to not take it, and to get back at her. Everyone could see she had problems, and he's so much bigger than her; but the crowd is giving their approval for him to get his revenge, and he does. They're all cheering him on, and I'm the only one trying to pull him away from her. The train stops and they both run off. The whole scene was disgusting. He should have known better, and so should have the crowd. He understandably let himself feel violated, and he let the crowd reconfirm his desire to extract his pound of flesh for his embarrassment. I walked away from there praying for everybody involved and hoping that had it happened to me; I would be strong enough to do the right thing.

Having made us in His image, our Creator knows us so well; and what idiots we can be. I can just imagine him thinking "It will take these yo-yos forever to figure out how to live, so I better get involved here", and so He gives us **the 10 Commandments.**

Love God

1-I am the Lord your God: you shall not have strange gods before me.

2-You shall not take the name of the Lord your God in vain.

3-Remember to keep holy the Lord's Day.

Love your neighbor

4-Honor your father and your mother.

5-You shall not kill.

6-You shall not commit adultery.

7-You shall not steal.

8-You shall not bear false witness against your neighbor.

9-You shall not covet your neighbor's wife.

10-You shall not covet your neighbor's goods.

These are *not* the *highest* things we shoot for. They are the *minimum* things needed for any communal life to retain any humanity.

Jesus' two Commandments

Then Jesus says "maybe 10 is too complicated for their simple minds; let me condense the whole 10 into 2":

1-You shall love God with all your heart, with all your soul, with all your mind, and with all your strength

2-You shall love your neighbor as yourself.

The Beatitudes

Then Jesus realizes "Hold it, these people have no clue about how to live a happy and blessed life; I better tell them". So Jesus gave us the Beatitudes:

1-Blessed are the poor in spirit,
  for theirs is the kingdom of heaven.
2-Blessed are they who mourn,
  for they will be comforted.
3-Blessed are the meek,
  for they will inherit the land.
4-Blessed are they who hunger & thirst for righteousness,
  for they will be satisfied.
5-Blessed are the merciful,
  for they will be shown mercy.
6-Blessed are the clean in heart,
  for they will see God.
7-Blessed are the peacemakers,
  for they will be called children of God.
8-Blessed are they who are persecuted for the sake
      of righteousness,
  for theirs is the kingdom of heaven.

The Holy Spirit Life

When we follow God's law and give our hearts, souls, and lives to Jesus, we live a life in the Holy Spirit.

What are the qualities of a person living in the *Fast Lane*?

There are gifts given to those who live in the spirit of Jesus:

The 7 Gifts of the Holy Spirit

1-wisdom   2- understanding

3- right judgment   4- courage

5- knowledge   6- reverence.

7- wonder and awe

How does a person living in the *Fast Lane* impact on others and their world?

There are specific qualities the person living in God's spirit has within them and spreads to the world around them:

The 12 Fruits of the Holy Spirit:

1-love   2-joy

3-peace   4-patience

5-kindness   6-goodness

7-generosity   8-gentleness

9-faithfulness   10-modesty

11-self control   12-chastity

Holy Mass

The holy sacrifice of the Mass is an essential part of the *Fast Lane* life. Worshiping God in the way that Jesus left behind for us is the most beautiful and important of human actions. The Eucharist is a portal of incredible graces and blessings. Here are some ways to breathe new life into the mass for yourself:

* Remember: Eucharist really is the most loving, amazing, supernatural event on earth. Bread and wine become the body and blood of Jesus
* Focus on what you will *give* to the celebration: sing, open doors, say the responses, be generous in your sign of peace, serve as an altar server, lector, extraordinary minister of Holy Communion, usher or welcoming ministry, connect with babies and little children
* go early and pray the rosary for those who will be attending
* focus on learning one thing that you can take home with you to use in your life
* refuse to allow things like bad music, boring homily, people coughing, sneezing or farting to get to you
* Experience mass celebrated in a different language or culture
* Try daily mass. It might be hard enough for you to go once a week; never mind every day. Give it a try. You'll see why so many people make it a goal and priority
* bring some snacks or a few boxes of donuts to give out to people after they leave church

The Repairs
There is wear and tear on us to be expected on the pilgrimage of life; the way travel takes a toll on any vehicle. How can we make repairs that will keep us moving in the *Fast Lane* on the road of life?

Rocky Road
First, don't expect life to be easy; the road of life is challenging and often difficult. Life is hard. All meaningful growth comes through pain, insight, love. There are plenty of **harsh realities** that are part of the journey:

1- Everyone you will ever love will die (no one lives on this earth forever)

2- Everyone you will ever count on will let you down (Only God is perfect)

3- Everything and everybody is always changing, and change is messy. Trying to possess people, and even moments in time, is futile because nothing is really yours. (Not every relationship lasts forever. Some are for a time.)

4- You accomplish nothing alone. The love and prayers of human and spiritual beings are part of everything that is happening. (Don't be so quick to take credit).

5- No one knows exactly how you feel; and you will never know exactly how someone else feels. We can know *something* about what each other feels; but because each of us is a unique collection of experiences and thought patterns which form emotions, our feeling states are never identical. (Respect individuality.)

6- No one will respond to every set of circumstances exactly the way you would. People act according to their level of investment; and no one cares about what you do exactly the same way you do. (Do what you must.)

7- "Death & taxes" You're going to die & while you're alive someone will make you pay. (Jesus says give them what they require; but be sure to give to God what is Gods'.)

8- There are people who will attempt to suck you dry; to take advantage of what you have achieved, and what you have been given, for their own benefit. (Don't hate them.)

9- Love hurts. Not everyone wants your love, and even fewer will return it. (Don't let anyone stop you from loving.)

10- You don't wait for everyone else to get their act together or care about something as much as you do. (Create the world you want to live in.)

Have Faith & keep Hope

A life with no God connection is like going off on a long trip with bald or nearly flat tires. At the very least you will get lousy mileage, and at the worst you could die and/or kill others in an accident caused from a tire blowout.

"The main thing is to keep the main thing, the main thing"

Two of the poorest places in the world that I have visited have huge statues of Jesus overlooking them. To me they represent what I've seen in my travels time and time again; how people that struggle and suffer greatly are sustained by deep faith and hope in the Lord.

Cochabamba Bolivia

Dili, East Timor

The greatest of these is Love

Have faith in love. Love is not a *nice* thing to do; it is the *only* thing to do. Love is the law of the universe, and when we love, we are in synch with the Creator; aligning our actions with His actions. Love trumps intelligence, creativity, and everything else. When love is united with our thoughts, emotions, imagination, and actions, amazing things can happen. *Without* love they are worthless. There are so many misconceptions about what love is and isn't. Love is not a warm mushy feeling. *Love is working for someone else's well-being as much as you would for your own.*

If that is the definition; ask yourself: Is there now; has there ever been, someone you can say you truly love or have loved?

Be willing to look at: do you *really* love them or do you love what they do for you?

Real love has nothing to do with what the other person is willing to receive or return. If by this definition, you are disappointed in yourself, let that be a motivation; but don't get stuck there. It's in the past. Right now you can commit yourself to true love from now on.

Live in the present moment

Notice it reads live "in" the present, **not** "for" the present. They are two different worlds. Being here, now is crucial; for each new moment is where the Holy Spirit lives and flows. Being fully alive in the here & now; means that *yesterday does not equal tomorrow.* Waiting for a better tomorrow to start really living is a waste of life. In each new moment is the potential for God and you to create something new

There is a story about a guy who wanted to be a Broadway star in the worst way. He finally gets his big chance; a small part, with only one line. It's a scene on a ship that has come under attack, and his line is "Hark, I hear the cannons roar". He is so grateful for the opportunity, and he rehearses it over and over: "Hark, I hear the cannons roar". "Hark, I hear the cannons roar". "Hark, I hear the cannons roar". Finally opening night comes and the play is unfolding. He knows when and where he is supposed to be on stage, and he's waiting for his moment when a loud boom occurs. He yells out at the top of his lungs "what the F#@! was that?"

It's not enough to know all the right lines, you have to be alive in the moment to know when and how to use them. It's easy to lose our way. It means remembering that this is all that is real right now: you are reading this book, and I am speaking with you through the words on this page. And most of all the God who created both of us is working through this process. And this is true for every moment you will ever live. Yesterday is gone; and tomorrow is not here yet. It's been said: ""Yesterday is history, tomorrow is a mystery, and today is a gift, that's why they call it the present."

Pray

It is important to pray honestly, openly and frequently. Pray from your heart; always keeping it real with God about whatever is going on with you. It's also important to pray when you don't feel like it. Abbot & Costello's comedy routine "Who's on First?" is a hysterical classic example of a communication breakdown. The same thing can easily happen between God and us. God never stops speaking to us; but we can easily get distracted or go off on another track, and can't even hear his voice anymore. The most serious handicap in life is to not be able to hear the voice of God speaking to you in your own heart, and within the experiences of your life. This is why prayer is so crucial for a true life with God.

Prayer, like all good communication, involves both speaking and listening. It is not just rattling off your little list of what you think God should be doing. He is the Lord of the universe, and doesn't need our advice. A friend of mine, who is not religious says that ultimately all prayer comes down to "now what?" Prayer is aligning your thoughts with God's thoughts. It is crucial for you to be able to love; which is aligning your actions with God's actions.

You CAN change

One of the parishes I consider home is St. Patrick in Long Island City in Queens, New York City. At the end of my first year there, the kids asked if I would coach their baseball team. I didn't hesitate: "NO". They were shocked "we thought you loved us". "I do; that's why I said no". I explained to them that I love baseball. I've watched it. I've played it. I never coached it. They needed someone who could *coach*. They explained to me that they once had a coach; but he felt he couldn't do anything more with them. They explained that without an adult, they would not be allowed to enter the league.

I understood what they were trying to do. They lived in a bad neighborhood; there was little to do but get into trouble: drinking, drugs, gangs, stealing. They were trying to keep busy and stay out of trouble, and I respected that. So I agreed to be their coach. Five minutes into the first practice I began to understand why the other coach might have dumped them. Not only did some of them not play very well; they weren't good at listening or paying attention.
Between all of that, and me not knowing much, we only won one game all season; and I think the only reason we won that game was because there was something wrong with the umpire (as in stoned or drunk). In the playoffs we, the last place team, were up against the first place team. You could not ask for a a more lopsided matchup. The first place team was a stacked team; 150 kids had tried out and they took the best 15.

On the other hand, I took anybody. Playing with the Queens Bombers was the only fun to do in that neighborhood that summer. As long as you weren't too old; I took you. You had one arm, half a leg, you could be on my team. Little brothers wanted to be with their older brothers. I had 9 year olds in a 14 year old league.

Before the playoff game I pulled my guys aside and reminded them that if we lost in the first round of the playoffs; that it would be the end of our season. There would be no more chances. I said "How about we win.

How about we pull the upset of the century. I believe in you guys; I think you can do it." They got fired up; even willing to say a prayer, ran onto the field and killed them 10-5. They were stunned that they had pulled it off, and went on to beat everyone else and became the New York City Y.M.C.A. champs that summer.

For them, and for me as well, it was one of the most miraculous experiences of our lives. It was also a great example of how change is possible; but only if the attitude changes first. All season long my guys would get down on themselves, and they didn't play very well. In the playoffs they saw themselves as champions, started to play better, and they became champions.

I know it sounds like a Disney movie, so I'm including the newspaper article. (In fact there is a baseball movie called "Hardball" based on an also true story of a team from Chicago. Our stories are almost identical; it's uncanny how so many of the details are the same. In fact when the movie was released, friends who knew of my story would tell me "Tony, they ripped off your life. Keanu Reeves is playing you!"

LIC Parish Team Takes YMCA Baseball Title

Sports

BY LEONARD KLIE

THE QUEENS BOMBERS, which are affiliated with St. Patrick's parish, Long Island City, overcame a 1-6-1 season to capture the YMCA Pirate Division baseball championship in late August.

The team, which started its season in May on a rocky footing, defeated its opposition, handily throughout the playoffs to lay claim to the title.

To reach the finals, the team had to dispose of the undefeated, top-seeded "A" team from the Immaculate Conception Youth Program, another Catholic parish-affiliated team. ICYP dominated league play all season and topped the Bombers in their previous meeting, 31-7. The Bombers did not want a repeat of that performance, and so they came in charged up. Led by pitcher Freddie Garcia, the Bombers jumped to an early lead and never looked back on their way to a decisive 10-5 win.

The victory earned the Bombers the right to go to the finals, where they would

Repent

Be willing to look at the sides of who you are as a person that are not of God. You were made to be in God's likeness; so that when people are

> **AN ACT OF CONTRITION**
> **Dear God with all my heart I am sorry for offending you,**
> **and I hate all my sins, most of all because they offend you my God; who are all good and deserving of all my love. I firmly resolve with the help of your grace to confess my sins, to make up for them**
> **and to change my life. Amen**

with you, more than anything, they see and meet God. *Our purpose is to magnify the presence of God in this world.* Without beating yourself up unnecessarily- be willing to repent for your sins. Be willing to shed a tear of sorrow for misusing the gifts you have been given including life itself and this world.

Make a good confession & receive the Sacrament of Reconciliation. If you have ever had a bad experience, try someone else. Remember that a priest can never reveal what you confess.

Let this conscience examination be a guide:

Do I love God above everything else?

Do I live as a child of God, confident in the Father's mercy?

Am I humble? Do I depend on God as I should?

Am I prideful? Do I try to make the world revolve around me?

Do I live out a sense of self -sufficiency, imposing my will on others, acting as if I were the cause of good in my life?

Do I think I can do whatever I want and that it will not matter to God?

Do I yearn to know God's will and do I abandon myself to divine Providence moment by moment?

Do I pray everyday? Do I go to Mass every Sunday and Holy Days?

Do I devote myself to growing in faith?

Am I thankful? Do I express my gratitude sincerely and outwardly, especially in works of mercy?

Do I make excuses for my faults, blame others, rationalize, or relativize?
Am I self-righteous?
Am I forgiving? Do I harbor grudges, resentments - do I take delight in the misfortunes of others?

Do I judge others, label others, exclude others, and condemn others?
Is my life in any way ruled by anger, jealousy, envy, or impatience?

Do I make gods of money, power, prestige, accomplishment, materialism, sensuality, vanity, pleasure, comfort, leisure, complacency, apathy, or anything else?

Do I put myself first through self-centeredness, egoism, selfishness, vanity, self-aggrandizing, etc.

Do I engage in premarital sex? Do I use sex recreationally?

How's my driving?

Do I dedicate myself to knowing, loving, and living the Truth as it is taught by the Catholic Church?

Do I live in the Truth and do I tell the truth, always & without compromise?

Do I misuse speech through cheating, gossiping, backbiting, profanity, blasphemy, complaining, being silent when I should speak, etc.?

Is my mind filled with thoughts that are lustful, viscous, carnal, mean-spirited, prejudicial, venal, worldly, etc.?

Do I waste time? Am I generous with my time? Am I lazy?

Do the priorities. in my life reflect and serve the precious gift of faith God has given me? Do I love more for myself than for God and others?

Do I live by faith or by emotions, by worldly philosophy, by current fads, by popular ideologies, by the pressures and deceptions of media and culture?

Do I recognize how God is present & active in every moment of my life? Do I live by any standard other than the way of love revealed by Jesus Christ?

Attitude of Gratitude

The surest sign that a person is living in the Holy Spirit is how often during the course of the day they find themselves in awe at the privilege given to them of being able to live a human life. With all the pain, suffering, disappointment, & frustration that goes with the human experience, it is all still such an amazing gift, beyond what we could ever imagine or deserve.

> A popular blessing before meals:
> *Bless us O Lord and these your gifts which we are about to receive from your bounty through Christ our Lord. Amen.*

Anyone who thinks they are worthy of heaven is crazy. Heck, I'm not worthy of THIS life. The blessing and privilege and gift of the chance to live a human life is too much. How could I possibly go through this life with an attitude of "I deserve this", never mind the audacity to believe that I deserve the afterlife with God Himself.

Simple ways to begin bringing more gratitude into your life: *never eat a meal without first giving thanks to God* for the blessing of something to eat; including in public places too. Remember you live on a planet where 1 in 8 people go to bed hungry.

> For food, in a world where so many walk in hunger.
> For faith, in a world where so many walk in fear.
> For Family & friends, in a world where so many walk alone.
> **We give thanks!**
> *Blessing before meal said in the film "7 Days in Utopia"*

Give thanks every night for the day you just lived & all your blessings.

Forgiveness & Mercy

At the juvenile detention facility I volunteer at, many young people are trying to rebuild their lives. They may have dealt drugs, assaulted, sexually abused, robbed, murdered, even murdered their own family. No matter what their crime; I have given every one of them a message of hope that it is possible in Christ to make a new beginning. They may have to pay a price for their actions; but inside they can be free in the love and mercy of the God who made them. This mercy is there for all of us.

One of the most powerful things you can do to energize your soul is to let go of a grudge. Holding onto resentments is like peeing on yourself; *no one feels it but you.* You are the one who gets hurt; not the person you're withholding love from. We are immersed in an ocean of God's love and mercy generously given to all of us, and to stay living in that flow, we are supposed to extend that mercy to others. The last thing you want to do is try to build barriers in the middle of that ocean, preventing it from flowing through and around you by caving into resentment. Block that flow and you will pay a terrible price.

One of the saddest times of my life was when a good friend of mine took his life. When he was fourteen, I had prepared him for his Confirmation. I made it a point to stay connected and support him after he received the sacrament. He had always had a rough life, and two years to the day after his older brother committed suicide, he took his life.

I was devastated; I felt I had failed him. He had been a member of the parish youth community, been on lots of retreats, and now he was gone. I was so upset; that I almost didn't go to the wake. But I knew that there would be a lot of people there needing comfort and support; so I went.

When I arrived at the funeral home, there was a bunch of his friends standing outside. I know all these guys so I'm hanging out with them, and listening to them vent. They were filled with shock, hurt, and anger. They were looking for someone to blame; and they seemed to agree it was the girlfriends fault. They blamed her for all the pain and trouble she had put him through; for getting him mixed up with the wrong people, temptations, bad habits, for cheating on him, and breaking his heart. Someone even said: "she dares to show up here, we kill her". They all grunted their agreement, and I'm saying to myself: "I sure hope she doesn't show!"

Just minutes later I see out of the corner of my eye, the girlfriend is coming down the path from the parking lot towards the funeral home. All the other guys see her too. Half of them walk away in the opposite direction; I think knowing if they stuck around they would do something they'd regret later. The other half are standing there fidgeting with their hands in their pants and jacket pockets. I know what these guys pack, and I'm looking around for backup only to realize there is no one out there but this girl, these guys and me. If someone is going to have to prevent something violent from happening here it has to be me. I'm frantically trying to take their eyes away from her, ridiculously calling their attention to the moon, the stars, anything.

Finally I hear the screen door of the funeral home open, and I'm relieved- finally someone else! Then I look and see that it is the mother of my friend who passed away. She came outside to smoke a cigarette. When I see that she has noticed the girlfriend; I'm thinking "Oh great- they're not going to have to kill her; the mother is going to do it."

The mother comes right down the steps, brushes past all of us, and goes right up to the girl. She puts her arm around her shoulder; and holding her tight to herself, comes back again past us almost defiantly, as if she could read everyone's minds. She goes up the steps and into the funeral home. We all follow, as the mother and girlfriend walk right down the aisle to the coffin, where they kneel down together. My friend's mother holds the girl in a tight embrace; letting her cry on her shoulder. Hand in hand, they pray the rosary together; and we all stand there in wonder; "How can this be happening?" Granted, it's not right to scapegoat somebody for a tragedy like this; but this woman knew how much agony this girl had put her son through, and yet by her actions she is showing that she holds no hatred, rejection or condemnation towards her at all. How?

At the end of the night I went up to her and told her "all my life I had been told that God forgives; and I learned it in my head. Tonight I learned it in my heart, because I SAW God forgive through you. No mother could do what you did unless God was working through you."

She simply smiled at me and said "wouldn't it really be something, if we could just be as good to each other as God is with us."

New York City Police Officer Steve McDonald miraculously survived being shot by a young man; but it paralyzed him. Ever since then he has been in a wheelchair, hooked up to a breathing machine. He forgave that kid, and has spent his whole life since it happened spreading around the world a message of hope through forgiveness and reconciliation.

In so many ways Steve is an inspiring man of God. I will never forget how when he heard that the youth I work with were having a walk-a-thon to raise money to help the poor; he came with us the whole way in his wheelchair alongside with us through the streets to help those who struggle and suffer in this world.

One of the most famous witnesses to the beauty and power of reconciliation, was when Pope John Paul II embraced and forgave the man who shot and nearly killed him.

We are often unable to forgive because we believe that to forgive means that we are saying that what the other person did was OK. *It Wasn't OK!* What it *does* mean is that we are letting go of bitterness and resentment, and putting the person in God's hands.

If you want to do one single thing today to free up tremendous spiritual energy to live your life with more passion and power, then let go of a grudge. I promise you this works. I also promise you that I know how difficult it can be to do this. I am very proud to be of Albanian heritage. We are a passionate people. I can also admit that if there is one thing we Albanians know how to do; it's carry a grudge. I have had to battle with it all my life. So when I say this is important to do; it's not something I say easily; but still know it to be true.

Among the greatest regrets we will have at the end of our lives will be the times when we did not have enough mercy towards others.

Who do *you* need to forgive?

Fasting

Denying yourself physically really helps the soul develop and creates a powerful ripple effect on the spiritual level of reality. Fasting from everything, but bread and water, once or twice a week is something that many people do to help them gain control over their body's desires. Don't fast for an extended time without consulting a health professional.

Sacrifice

Offering up something frees us from being controlled by it. By sacrificing our money, time, or energy we discipline ourselves, and learn how to count on God, instead of ourselves and the things we are attached to. Sacrifice also has great power on the spiritual level, and every sacrifice makes a difference. The saying "offer it up for the souls in purgatory" expresses how our sacrifices affect others, and the whole of reality.

Be led by Jesus

If you ever get an chance, definitely volunteer to help out with the Special Olympics. They are Olympic style events for people with special needs. The way it usually works is that you adopt one person with special needs for the day. You become their coach; and they tell you that your responsibility is to help make sure they have a good experience.

The first time I volunteered for the Special Olympics they gave me Byron, who was twenty years old, but mentally about three. I was told he could be a handful; but I found him to be an easy-going fun-loving guy. He was really enjoying all the food, and joking around with me about how any medals he was going to win. Then it came time for his race. They announced "everyone running the fifty yard dash report to the track." I said "Byron that 's your race, lets go". Suddenly all the joy ran out of his face, and he was looking really sad and uncomfortable. I told him: "Hey Byron, don't worry, you don't have to win, we'll just run around a little bit. It'll be fun". Nothing seemed to give him any comfort. When they called his name to report to the starting line. I tried again to get him excited "hey Byron that's you!". He looked terror stricken.

Then he began to shake. I remembered it said on his chart that he could have seizures. I began to feel like a failure. Not only is he not having a good time, now he's going to freak out. Nothing I said was making any difference; but finally I got an idea. I said "Byron, this is what we're going to do: I'm going to go down to the finish line down there and I'll be standing with my arms open. You just run straight to me. Run straight to me ok?" I left the starting line and began running to the finish line. I stopped to look back, and make eye contact with him. But I didn't know he had been following me, and when I turned around he ran right into me and we both fell to the ground. There we were in front of all these people lying there on the track. I helped pull him up and said "no, Byron, you have to wait till the gun goes off. Go back and wait until the gun goes off."

I got to the finish line I yelled out a few times "remember Byron, run straight to me". The gun went off, and he was running at full speed. He ran into my arms, and won the race and the gold medal; and most importantly, the smile came back on his face.

I learned something. As I was saying to Byron "run straight to me" I felt Jesus saying those words to *me*. I had been worried about what Byron would do when the gun went off. Would he run back up into the stands? Would he run in the opposite direction? Or worst of all would he run sideways and knock everybody over? But once I said "THIS is the way, and I'll be there for you"; he knew exactly where to go, what to do, and he could be confident knowing that he was not alone.

That's who Jesus is to us. His arms stretched open wide on the cross says "I love you, I'm here for you. You're not alone. This is the way. Run straight to me".

Jesus knows how hard it is for any of us, especially a young person, today to follow the right road. There are so many temptations and distractions; so many voices screaming at you demanding your time and attention, and telling you how to live. Most of them have no concern at all for what is right and truly best for you. So Jesus puts Himself front and center and says: "stay focused on Me and you'll always know what to do."

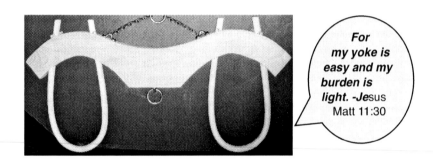

> For my yoke is easy and my burden is light. -Jesus
> Matt 11:30

In Jesus' time, and in many countries around the world even today, yokes are used to keep together two animals pulling a cart or plow or whatever is needed. An experienced animal, who knows what to do and how to lead, is paired up with one that is less experienced, who basically only has to follow. Jesus is saying to us, "let Me lead". Life is easier and lighter when we let Him lead us; because He knows the way.

Be Faithful
Mother Teresa often said that "God has not called us to be successful. He has called us to be faithful". Know that

God tests our faithfulness in small things before He can give us the big opportunities.

The summer before I was about to start a youth ministry in Queens Village, I moved there, (and actually still live there to this day). I had hoped that I could use the summer months to be visible and make connections; but it seemed the only kid that wanted to bother with me was this one teen, who had gotten some bad drugs, and had a mental breakdown. The medication he was on caused him to always be hungry. All he ever wanted to do was eat, and he was lonely. So I would go out to eat at fast food restaurants with him almost every day for that whole summer. I know that had I not been faithful to that one kid; God never would have blessed me to build with Him one of the largest youth ministries ever in America.

When I turned the first floor of my home into a performance space and art gallery, and began to have shows; there was a guy from the neighborhood who would come regularly. His poetry and songs were definitely *different*; but I knew that welcoming him was a test. I know that if I had not been kind, encouraging and welcoming to him; I would not have been blest with all these years of hundreds of people coming to my place, and all the fun and performances I've enjoyed.

Convert

Constantly allow yourself to be changed. Little kids are always learning, growing and taking new chances. *Be that way*. Be willing to put aside everything that is not of God. ***The main thing is to keep the main thing the main thing***. The main thing is that no one gets to live in their body on this earth forever. We are all going home somewhere and when we get there, how we lived here matters. Ask Jesus to show you all the areas of your life that have not yet been given over to Him.

Spiritual Friends

Always remember that those who love you will never stop loving you. There are so many in heaven praying for you. There are family members that you never even met that pray for you every day.

Your Guardian Angel, your patron saint(s), the many angels and saints, Our Mother Mary, and most of all Jesus are praying for you and supporting you always.

Accept God's will

Things that appear to be ending are really just changing; and sometimes you can have no idea how something you feel called to do is going to go.

There was a show on Broadway called Blood Brothers. It featured Petula Clark, who is somebody I had a crush on in my youth, and the Cassidy Brothers, whom my sister had a crush on. I wanted to do something special for my sister and treat her to the show. I wanted her to feel comfortable with going, and not feel obligated to return the favor. So I told her that I knew somebody involved with the show, and I was able to get the tickets for a Sunday matinee (when I knew she could make it) for only $10.00, and since they were so cheap, I insisted on treating her.

She was so happy and excited, and proceeded to tell all my brothers and sisters about the incredible $10.00 Broadway seats. The next thing I know, they're all calling me to get themselves and their spouses and boyfriends and girlfriends in on the $10.00 seats which were really $60.00 each. I didn't want to say anything, to make sure that the original sister never found out the real price, so I had to buy 10 additional tickets. It turned out to be a great time for everybody, it just cost me a lot more than I planned on.

"If you want to make God laugh; tell him your plans.

You just never know how when you set something from your heart in motion, how it's going to turn out. Trust and accept that God will use what you create the way *He* wants. I was really blessed because, not only did I get to make my family, especially my sister, happy; after the show when we stuck around for my sister to get a glimpse of the Cassidy brothers leaving, she saw Petula Clark, and I got to meet her.

Community

You can't be a Christian alone. Fast Lane living is *never* "Me and my Jesus". Those who love God, He places in their hearts the desire to overflow that love into the world, into life and into the relationships of their life. Living in relationship and in community is messy; but it is the only way your soul can develop the way God wants it to.

We all need to belong. When I was in Ghana in remote villages; I found that people there had a glowing image of the United States. I was often asked, "do you have any problems at all there". I said "yes, we have many"; and when pressed to be specific, I mentioned homelessness. They couldn't believe it. Among those African people; everyone always has a home. There is always a family compound, a place you could return to be with people who consider your family. When they learned that in our society there are people, who don't belong anywhere, they literally cried for us. They could no longer respect us; because we live in such a way that many of our people have no place to call home.

This may be the great work of our lives at this time: to make the world a home again, a place where we live in communion, in community, creating an expression of the unity we will have in heaven. This is at least what the Church should be; the place where all are welcomed. You are a member of God's team, the Church. We need you. Together we can do what none of us can do alone.

One of my favorite monologues is from the film Any Given Sunday in which Al Pacino plays a football team coach. They're beating themselves by backstabbing each other. This is the locker-room speech where he is trying to turn things around before the big game by getting them to pull together.

I don't know what to say really.
Three minutes to the biggest battle of our professional lives
all comes down to today.
Either we heal as a team or we are going to crumble.
Inch by inch, play by play till we're finished.
We are in hell right now, gentlemen believe me
and we can stay here and get the s--- kicked out of us
or we can fight our way back into the light.
We can climb out of hell. One inch, at a time.
Now I can't do it for you. I'm too old.
I look around and I see these young faces and I think
I mean I made every wrong choice a middle age man could make.
I uh.... I pissed away all my money believe it or not.
I chased off anyone who has ever loved me.
And lately, I can't even stand the face I see in the mirror.
You know when you get old in life things get taken from you.
That's, that's part of life.
But, you only learn that when you start losing stuff.
You find out that life is just a game of inches. So is football.
Because in either game; life or football the margin for error is so small.
I mean one half step too late or to early you don't quite make it.
One half second too slow or too fast and you don't quite catch it.
The inches we need are everywhere around us.
They are in ever break of the game every minute, every second.
On this team, we fight for that inch
On this team we tear ourselves & everyone around us to pieces for that inch.
We CLAW with our finger nails for that inch.
Cause we know when we add up all those inches
that's going to make the difference
between WINNING and LOSING
between LIVING and DYING.
I'll tell you this-in any fight it's the guy who is willing to die
who is going to win that inch.
And I know if I am going to have any life anymore
it is because, I am still willing to fight, and die for that inch
because that is what LIVING is. The six inches in front of your face.
Now I can't make you do it.
You gotta look at the guy next to you.
Look into his eyes.
Now I think you are going to see a guy who will go that inch with you.
You are going to see a guy who will sacrifice himself for this team
because he knows when it comes down to it,
you are gonna do the same thing for him.
That's a team, gentlemen
and either we heal now, as a team, or we will die as individuals.
That's football guys. That's all it is. Now, whattaya gonna do?

How to be Happy

The way to be happy is to give your heart and your life to God. Ask the Holy Spirit to live in you, and live the life that flows out of that. Happiness starts with having a true friend, a companion who only wants what's best for you, and will never leave you or let you down. Let Jesus be that friend. Put knowing, loving and serving God first, above everything else, and you will be happy. There is no greater happiness than receiving the gifts of God and blessing the world by sharing them with everyone.

J esus first
O thers second
Y ou third

It's never too late to have a happy childhood!

No Matter What

Love as God loves; pouring everything out to others; without concern for what is coming back to you.

I became a teacher because I hated school as a kid. All the way through College I was disgusted and bored with the whole education system. At the end of college I got the idea that I should try my hand at teaching; and if I could do better than what was done to me, I would feel satisfied. If I couldn't; then I would just quietly accept that school has to be boring and irrelevant.

I was blessed to get a teaching job at all since I was only 22, and had never taken one single education course during my whole undergraduate studies. I was really enjoying being for my students the kind of teacher that I always wanted to have. My biggest difficulty was the principal, Sister Mary Edna. She was an older woman, who it seemed, thought everything I did was wrong. I was always in more trouble than my students. It really aggravated me. I was going all out for the students. They loved my classes. I started a school paper. I did retreats. I led after-school rap groups. I organized a show. Yet I was the teacher, who was always being called down to the office for something. It got to the point where I said to myself "I'm going to be the kind of teacher I want to be no matter what." I kept on like that for two years, until I left teaching to go into youth and parish work.

A few years later there was a retirement party for Sr. Mary Edna, and I didn't feel like going; except I really had to since I was part of the parish staff. At the party, when she saw me enter the room, she practically ran over to me, and with teary eyes said "I am so glad I got to meet you, and just remember: keep on doing what you've got to do, no matter what."

Then *I* got all teary as it hit me: what I learned from her was exactly what she was trying to teach me. She knew that for me to be me, I was going to have to be tough, and working for a person criticizing you everyday for everything you do that you think is right- well that will either toughen you up or drive you away. The love she had for me was like a parents' love. A parent that knows what their child needs and will push for that even if they are never appreciated or even resented for it- no matter what.

The Little things (*no such thing*)
Remember that the small details and the little things are not little, and down the line lead to greater things.

As an example, my own life follows these steps:

1- God placed within me a love for Him, the arts, and helping people.

2- I attend a conference combining the arts and spirituality.

3- There are hundreds of people there; one is a priest from Ghana who is a guest of someone attending.

4- He sees my work there with the teens, and invites me to work with the youth of his country.

5- I go.

6- I travel to remote villages. In some cases I am the first white man they have ever seen. Usually in those villages everyone comes out to greet me, and there is a party where they perform their talents: singing, dancing, drumming, sharing jokes and poetry. I'm amazed at how easily they all share what they can do.

7- I realize that where I live in America this never happens. I dream that one day I might start an opportunity for people back home to perform at the grassroots level.

8- Soon after, I turn the first floor of my home in Queens, New York City into a performance space called "the Vault".

9- Hundreds of people have the opportunity to perform on our stage.

Also from that same trip:

1- In one of those villages I also met a chief, begging me for help for his people.

2- Coming back home I mobilize my friends to be of assistance this to man and his village

3- I create Hope for the Children Foundation

4- tens of thousands of people are empowered by the work of the foundation at the grassroots level.

All of this started with the simple love of God, appreciation for art, and desire to help others, leading to one event, leading to one person, one trip and two major projects of my life.

It ain't over till it's over

I was at a Yankee game with my brother and my nephew. It was a tied game, and it got very exciting when late in the game it looked like the Yankees were going to break through with their big hitters. It was a boiling hot day; but everyone in the entire stadium was up on their feet, cheering, sure something big was going to happen. It didn't, and the game went into extra innings. The Yankees are up again and, to my surprise, the whole stadium is sitting down. I turn to my brother questioning how it could be, and he says to me "looks who's up!" It was Ricky Ledee. He had struck out several times that game, killing a few rallies. I think he may have dropped a ball or two in the outfield too; not his best day by any stretch.

In the middle of a quiet stadium, I yell out "Hey Ricky, prove 50,000 people wrong!" Right then he hit a walk off home run, winning the game. The whole crowd around us are staring at me wondering "how did he know?". I learned that day: *you don't give up on yourself or other people.* We're all one at-bat away from hitting it out of the park. When you're about to give up on something; that's often when a breakthrough happens- so don't actually give up; even though you may feel like it.

Laugh at yourself

Not taking yourself too seriously; keeps you in the Fast Lane.

One of my favorite places to visit for retreats every year is New Mexico. I love the people there; but sometimes wonder how they live there because it is also home to some of the smelliest places I travel to. Roswell; where supposedly space-ships crashed many years ago, has a sign at the entrance to town that says "Welcome to Roswell, dairy capital of the Southwest"; which I guess is a nice way of warning "our town smells like cow poop". I especially love Artesia, because they *really* have the ability to laugh at themselves. It's a small town, where nothing ever happens; and due to the oil refineries, dumps and cows, is probably the smelliest of all. They have these billboards at the entrances to their town.

Conspiracy of Accidents

It's been said that in this reality, divine providence, God's love, shows itself as a conspiracy of accidents. It was an icy cold January day in New York City, and all day long my friend Louie kept popping up in my head. Louie and I go way back. I was the first person he ever told that he was gay, and now all these years later he's suffering with AIDS in a hospital on Roosevelt Island, NYC. I'd just been to visit Louie for Christmas and so I'm a little surprised that I keep thinking about him; but it's so persistent that I decide to make the trip. I get there, and I can't believe what I'm seeing. Louie is laying in his hospital bed and can hardly breathe. He's in agony, literally fighting for every single breath. I'm shocked; I was *just* here, and he was fine. He was in good spirits. We were laughing, joking singing Christmas songs; and now he can't even breathe, never mind speak, laugh or sing.

I felt so useless. I didn't know what to do, except hold his hand, and try to radiate as much love as I could. In my heart was one prayer: "Lord please don't let him suffer like this much longer." Visiting hours ended, and the nurse tells me to leave. I kiss Louie on the forehead, tell him I love him, and walk out wondering: what was *that* all about? Why that overwhelming urge to go visit him? Why? So I could have one more experience under my belt of feeling helpless to do anything to relieve the suffering of someone I cared about?

I'm back home less than half an hour, when the hospital called to tell me that Louie had passed away.

Conspiracy of accidents?

When Louie came out as being gay it was a different time; well maybe for some people, not that different at all. He was pretty sure that I would not reject him like so many others ended up doing. When he came down with AIDS, there were only two people that stood by him. What I didn't know until later was that at the end, Louie's only other friend was on vacation a thousand miles away. For his last day on earth, if Louie was going to be able to be with someone he loved, and who loved him; in this whole world of billions of people there was only one person who that could have been. Coincidence? Conspiracy of accidents? You decide.

This is how the Holy Spirit works. Most of us have some experience in our lives when we were thinking about someone, and then they were on the phone, or at our door or friend requesting us on Facebook. We don't usually talk about these things much so we don't get labeled weird; but they happen and they are the way God often works. Follow through on those urges, especially if someone comes to mind while you're praying.

Dreams can also be another way the Holy Spirit leads us to where we are needed to be.

Never waste anything

Everything you have is gift; so appreciate it. Go through life never taking more than you need. Because you live in what is

> The world has enough for human need, but not enough for human greed.
> GANDHI

called a "consumer culture" you need to constantly evaluate what do you really need *vs.* what have you been programmed to believe you will be less than a successful human being if you don't have it. Remember: you are constantly being lied to about the requirements for a good life; so you can't make your decisions based on the propaganda, *and* you can't follow the crowd.

In reality you will *always* need less than you thought. Don't throw your excess away, donate it. You are surrounded by organizations who will help people in need make use of what you are letting go of.

Never throw food away.

Never waste water.

Turn lights & electric devices off when not needed.

Recycle paper, glass, cans etc.

Donate cellphones, eyeglasses, computers.

Follow your passion

When you combine your commitment to God and spreading His love and your God-given talents and passion, amazing things can happen.

Surf for the Cause

These friends of mine combine their 2 great passions: surfing and helping people. They realized that some of the best surf in the world is in poor countries. They don't want to just visit these countries, and take advantage of the good surf. While visiting they connect with the people, and make a difference improving the quality of their lives.

Performing Life Bolivia

John Connell; fresh out of high school, started this project to help kids who live and work in the streets of Cochabamba, Bolivia rebuild their lives. John's project has grown tremendously due to his talents, hard work, and love for and dedication to his street kids. He could settle for his successes, but he always reaches out to more youth who are still in need. He uses his creativity and love for the arts in his work: forming his street jugglers into a performance troupe, helping them make bracelets they can sell, and recording hip hop CDs.

Grassroots Films

My friends in Brooklyn NYC are great filmmakers and are a great example of how God works through people who have responded to His call. These guys use their skills to create life-changing art that touches people's hearts and souls.

Just to mention a few more;
Dr. Tony Lazzara, and Jean Louis Lebel in Peru,
John and Ledis Coronna in Nicaragua,
are also real heros I know personally, who dig their heels in where God has planted them, and make a difference at the grassroots level. They are showing all of us how you change the world with the power and love of God.

Integrity

Maintaining integrity in your word and actions is crucial for fast-lane living. To live a noble life requires that we speak and live by the highest ideals that Jesus gave us, and we know in our hearts to be true.

My best friend as a little kid was my Aunt Josie; the little old lady who lived next door. She wasn't related to us by blood; but closer to us than any relative. In her late 80's she fell and broke her hip. When my sister and I visited her in the hospital she was out of it. She meant everything to me; and I was upset that if this was the end for her; she might not experience my "I love you" for the

last time. I was praying that she would come to, and she did.

Do you know what we did then? We laughed. We went over all the funny, crazy things that had happened over the years. There were so many memories, the times we hid on her when she would babysit us. There was the time we were playing baseball in her yard, and broke her bathroom window, while she was in the bathroom, and she never told our mother. There were so many birthday parties where so many funny things happened. We just laughed and laughed.

The visiting hours ended; we hugged, kissed and expressed our love. As we left I remember saying to my sister, "I'll bet that's the last time we see her". Sure enough she passed away later that day.

I still miss my Aunt Josie. In some ways she is with me whenever I share her story on retreats, and she is here with me now as I give honor to her life by sharing this story with you. I always treasure the many little kindnesses she showed me as a kid, and I will always remember her last moments of life on earth; and what she wanted to do as her life was coming to an end.

She didn't want to go back over all the things she had accomplished. She had actually been out west in a covered wagon as a little girl. She was the first woman on Long Island to buy a car. She had seen many places and done many things. But those memories were not what she cared about.

She had worked until her late seventies. She was a secretary for some important people, and made decent money in an era when it was difficult for women to succeed. At the end, that wasn't what mattered.

What she wanted to do was celebrate the love she shared with me and my family. In her golden years we were her only family.

I often find myself remembering this little old woman leaving this life, and going on to the next; with a smile on her face, and joy in her heart. I see my Aunt Josie embraced by her Savior, ready for what He held next for her. I imagine her saying with integrity, "It was good that I lived. It was good that I loved these people and they loved me. We laughed together, and helped each other. We made life good, and beautiful, and happier for each other. I'm ready now."

I want that. I believe in your soul you want that too. This is life in the Fast Lane. Let the Holy Spirit guide you there.

Dream Big

You are in the world at a big time in human history. God has got to have given some, if not most of you, reading this book some big dreams. Go for them. Some of you will receive the support of those

> *"Some men see things as they are and say why. I dream things that never were and say why not." -Shaw*

closest to you. You don't wait for it. Often they will tell you you're crazy, and should be more realistic. They want to try and prevent you from getting hurt.

Sometimes you can have a big idea and you're not even sure why, or how it's going to play out. In 1992 I ran for President of the United States. I was an independent write-in candidate registered with the Federal Board of Elections. I didn't do very well. I lost money, couldn't get much media attention, and didn't have the votes or even support of those closest to me. I knew it was a crazy idea. I knew I might not win; still I wanted to use the campaign as a way to surface some issues about what's wrong with the world, and changes I thought needed to be made that none of the other candidates were talking about. I had prayed about it every day leading up to the campaign. I kept saying; "God this is crazy; but if you want me to do it, I will". I always got the same sense to go ahead with it.

You could say that it didn't turn out too well. You could even say it was a huge failure. Still, my campaign slogan "Hope for the Children" later became the name of the foundation I created to work for justice in the world. I also know that maybe someone reading this book feels they could do a better job of leading their country than the people in power now. Maybe hearing about how since *I* tried it, they can also do something that radical *(and fare a lot better!)*.

Everyone is worth it

We usually don't have full knowledge of the effects of our actions both for good, and not so good. Whenever the Holy Spirit is involved, and you put yourself and your actions in God's hands; trust that there is always a blessing for you, and for those you are giving to, even if it is not evident at the time.

I started an art and literary journal called "Soul Fountain". I receive art and poetry from all over the US and the world. I make it a point to include in the journal something from everyone who submits, whether I like their work or not; or feel that it is brilliant or not. For awhile one of the top poets in New York City edited the journal for me until I saw that he was very elitist in his attitude and actions regarding the journal, and I took it back.

My main goal with *Soul Fountain* is to give people, especially young and beginner poets, the joy of seeing something they created published. I got a package from man in Florida thanking me for including his poem. He told me how he had never been published before in his whole life; and he could now die happy having seen his work in print. I had no idea I had made such a difference in someone's life like that. Besides the joy of knowing I had brought him some happiness; there was an extra bonus. Many of the items in his package were very helpful and relevant for me. It was as if he knew me, and it was like getting a package from God.

I love my street kids in Cochabamba Bolivia. On a recent trip to visit them, one of our kids was celebrating his ninth birthday. John, who created and runs the project with the kids, makes sure everyone has a celebration of their birthday, including a huge birthday cake. I watched this little boy crying as he looks at his cake, and everyone is singing "Happy birthday". He's crying because it is the first time someone cared enough about him to celebrate his birthday, and give him a cake. If I do nothing else in my life, I was a part of helping one little boy feel so much joy that others cared about him, and celebrated with him that they were glad he had been born into this world.

Look inside, you know you were born to live like that. Strive to live your life in such a way that each day contains at least one moment where God worked through you and with you to touch one person.

Be Bold

Probably the biggest regrets in my life come from times when I played it safe; times when I should have confronted somebody, or stuck up for somebody.

I watched a mentally challenged young man having dinner in a restaurant with his parents during the

Christmas season. You could see how happy and proud he was to be having this dinner with them, and he's savoring every moment. It was also obvious that the parents did not want to be there. Their body language, facial expressions, and curt responses clearly showed that they were annoyed about this intrusion into their busy schedules. They focused on the food, and not on their son; giving him almost no eye contact. They made no attempts at conversation, and it seemed to me they were being outright rude to him.

He was either trying hard to be oblivious to their resentment, or he chose to ignore it; but every once in awhile he slipped, and I could see the hurt on his face, and sadness in his eyes over their rejection. Maybe he knew they didn't love him; but he was still so grateful for any little bit of time or attention he could get from them.

At the end of the meal the two parents handed their son the check and made a quick exit. First they treated him like like he was an annoyance, and then they made him pay. I wanted to get up and run after them. I wanted to just shake them and get right in their faces "what is wrong with you? Don't you know how lucky you are to have a son who loves you so much."
So many times I wish that I had done that. I know that opening my mouth would have probably been stepping out over some line of what's acceptable. I still wish I had stuck up for him.

Walking down a city street one night, I see up ahead a group of jocks from a local college. They were loud, and probably had been out drinking. One of them tripped over a homeless man in a doorway. They proceeded to kick the heck out of him, screaming "You Bum, get the f___ out of our way" and then ran off. I wanted to run after them and say "what the heck is wrong with you? That's a human being". I tried to help the homeless guy; but he was so frightened and shaken from the experience, he wouldn't let me do anything for him. I will never forget his huddled up body frozen from cold and fear. I should have gone after those guys. I might have been the next one to get beaten up on that night; but that would be OK.

I have also had some successes when I did take the bold action for others. When I was the youth minister in Queens Village, I twice brought the Punk Rock band *The Ramones* to play at my parish. It was a crazy thing to do; but I knew how much everyone loved *The Ramones*. To this day people still smile when they talk about how they saw *The Ramones* play at Our Lady of Lourdes in Queens Village.

Mysterious Ways

In my travels I often meet people, who are sure they have seen me before. Some recognize me from a"Duralube" commercial and infomercial. It was the corniest thing I ever did as an actor; but it is also the most widespread. In the program they treat this humungous engine with Duralube. Then they drain all the oil out, and it still runs. Then they drain all the water out, and it still runs. Then they put water in the distributor cap treated with Duralube, and it still runs. Then the firemen drench the entire engine with this fire hose, and it still runs. I'm the guy who says; "If I didn't see it; I wouldn't believe it." Yeah that's me. I played a Taxi driver; which I really was at the time. I'm also the guy who says "No oil, no water, water in the electrical system, water all over the place, next thing you'll be telling us you that with Duralube you won't even need gasoline to run this thing." Then there was my dramatic account of how Duralube helped get me through the "Storm of the Century".

Yep that's me. I wish I had a dollar for every time that thing has aired. It seems everyone who knows me has seen it. Even my half blind, half out-of-it Grandmother saw it. (Why she was watching a program about a motor oil additive, I'll never know. The woman never drove a car a day in her life.) It blows my mind how many people will sit down and watch something like that between two and six in the morning. I got so many messages: "It's three in the morning, and you're on my TV- What is going on?" "Duralube ,huh Tone? Career is really moving ahead I guess." "What are you doing infomercials like that for?" And of course I have always countered with: "what kind of life do *you* have, that you have a half hour to kill watching things like that?"

Of course the big question was always; "hey Tony does the stuff really work?"

At eighteen years old I started my first youth group at my parish. Ray was one of the teens who joined us. He had serious problems at home. We welcomed him, and he considered us family. He came to every event we had; all the trips, meetings, retreats, and parties.

When I moved out on my own, I invited him to come along, and I saw it as a chance to be like a big brother, looking after him. It turned out Ray had an alcohol and drug addiction that I had been blind to. At that time I was very naive and uninformed about how to help an addicted person. It ended up very badly with him stealing from me and running away. I didn't see or hear from him for many years until a surprise phone call. He told me how he had drank and drugged for the nearly twenty years since I had last seen him.

He told me how he ended up down South, and had a time when he hit rock-bottom. He had enough of life, and with a knife ready in his hand, was going to end it all. He screamed out to God to give him a reason to stay alive. He wondered if there was any hope for him ever having a decent, happy life. He told God this was the time to send a sign before he took his life. He laid on that kitchen floor waiting for an answer from God.

The only thing that came to him were the memories of our youth group; a time when he was loved, accepted and happy. He thought it was unusual that he should recall those days; since he had not thought about them in ages. The good memories didn't really change the circumstances of his life; but he did feel better enough to put the knife away.

He told me how it was two in the morning, and he walks into his living room now and turns on the TV and what do you think is showing? My face in the Duralube program! And if he should have any doubt about it being me, because he hasn't seen me in 20 years; it's the part that says "Tony Bellizzi- taxi driver".

For him it was like Jesus was right there in his living room. He's thinking "what are the chances?" I'm going to end my life and this guys pops up in my head, and now here he is on my TV!"

The next day he checked himself into a rehab and changed his whole life. I recently met his mother at a parish mission I was conducting, and she told me that Ray had recently gone home to heaven; but before he died he had made his peace with God and his family.

So if you're wondering if the product works?- Yes- but in mysterious ways!

My whole acting training and career was worth it; if for nothing else to help save Ray's life. You never know how God in his glory will use your actions down the line to work a miracle.

Learn to listen to your inner voice, the part of you that knows when something is an invitation from God, and he needs you to go somewhere and do something, even and *especially* if there is a big part of you that would rather not do it.

Road trips

Journeys with Jesus
(Fast Lane Adventures)

Adoration

Visit a church, where you can sit before the Blessed Sacrament. There is a great peace, strength and many graces that come from being the presence of Jesus Himself. Allow yourself just BE with Him. Resist the temptation to cut it short by checking your phone.

Are we having fun yet?

Joy and laughter are the most definite signs of the presence of God. God definitely has a sense of humor- *He made us!* In our laughter, we give God glory and it also heals. They say "laughter is the best medicine".

Road trips:

*Make a collection of the funny stories & cartoons you come across. Share them on Twitter & Facebook.
* Make the most of April Fools Day & Halloween
* Check out: Onion magazine & website, Mad Magazine, Funny Side monthly comedy magazine
* Enjoy comedy movies, TV sitcoms, YouTube & websites, Comedy Central, Late night TV
* Great comics like George Carlin, Lee Camp, and Ted Alexandro have an ability to see so many things about life so clearly, radically, and also be hysterically funny. (no-I don't approve of all of the language)

You don't think you're personally funny? Then notice & share when something or someone else is funny.

Have as much fun in this life as possible, and never follow a humorless leader.

<u>*See the fun in everyday kind of moments:</u>* (*just to name a few*)

*If you left some kind of food on your face and someone points it out say: "I'm saving it for later".

*Someone asks for your help say "I'm on vacation" (then help them of course)

*If someone asks you a question answer "well the __*th* rule of Fight Club says___"

*think of funny ways to use movie lines in everyday conversation

Art

Experiencing and creating art has the power to touch the soul. God made us in His image. When we create we are imitating our Creator. Co-creating with Him is what we are made for. What art-form do you enjoy the most? What & whose art moves you; expressing and inspiring the spiritual? Is there an artistic talent you used to have but have forgotten or ignored? Guided by the Holy Spirit; how might you more frequently use your artistic talent to give glory to God? Don't just be a passive consumer of culture; create something: *a painting, poem, story, screenplay, a video, a movie, a sculpture, a scrapbook, a song.*

Blast from the past

Check out how a childhood friend is doing. Pay a visit to a friend or relative you haven't seen in ages. Especially follow through if someone pops up in thoughts or prayers.

Brave New World

Immerse yourself in another culture. Spend a portion of your summer or some other vacation break on a mission trip to a developing nation or with people in need in your own country. Go there to work, and don't treat it as a vacation. Get your hands dirty and lose yourself in service: "it's not about you!" Learn from and interact with the people and refrain from judging. Be an explorer not a tourist.

Christmas is the best time of the day

Christmas provides opportunities for sharing in the crazy abundance of God's love. Why wait all year? Every day try to do something unexpectedly and anonymously for someone else. Be outrageously generous with your time, talent, money and gifts.

Comfort the disturbed, disturb the comfortable

Which one of these are you more like these days- disturbed or comfortable? Be willing to ask God to give you what you need to either shake you up or heal you. See what happens!

Second step- pray for the people God has placed in your life; that they find solace or challenge at this time in their life. Be open to being an instrument.

Dream

Dreams are a powerful way God shows you things. We can learn a lot through dreams because they often bring out the things we don't deal with during our waking hours. Many people find it helpful to keep a dream journal.

Encourage a Friend

Take the time and make the effort to offer your prayers, support and encouragement to friends who are facing struggles, temptations, or difficult situations. Sometimes we just need to know someone else also recognizes what we know is the difficult but right thing to do.

Exercise

Exercise is a great way to care for your body and your soul. God made our bodies in such a way that He works well through us when our bodies are in motion. Make time for some physical activity every day. Organize a game, take a hike, join a gym, run, walk, skateboard, swim.

Facebook etc.

Social networking is a tool; use it for good; to laugh & love
* Wish people happy birthday.
* post humorous photos, videos
* post inspirational quotes & videos
* respond to postings expressing some need for love

Father's Love Letter

Read this letter of love from your heavenly Father. Your Creator wants you to know how special you are to Him.
My Child,

You may not know me, but I know everything about you...	Ps 139:1
I am familiar with all your ways...	Psalm 139:3
For you were made in my image. ..	Genesis 1:27
In me you live and move and have your being...	Acts 17:28
You are my offspring.. .	Acts 7:28
I knew you even before you were born.. .	Jer :4-5
I chose you when I planned all of creation...	Eph 1:11-12

You were not a mistake, for all your days are written in my book... Ps 139
I determined the exact time you would be born & where you would live. Acts 17:-26

You were wonderfully made...   Psalm 139:14
I knit you together inside your mother's womb..   Psalm 139"13
And brought you forth on the day you were born...   Psalm 71:6
I have been misrepresented by those who don't know me... Jn 8:4I-44
I am not distant and angry, but am the complete expression of love...   1Jn4:16
And it is my desire to lavish my love on you...   1John 3:1
Simply because you are my child and I am your father... 1John 3:1
I offer you more than your earthly father ever could... Matthew 7:11
For I am the perfect father...   Matthew 5:48
Every good gift that you receive comes from my hand.. .James 1:17
I am your provider and I meet all your needs... Matthew 6:31-33
My plan for your future has always been filled with hope. ..Jer29: I
Because I love you with an everlasting love... Jeremiah 31:3
My thoughts toward you are countless as the sand on a seashore. Ps 139
I will never stop doing good to you...   Jeremiah 32:40
For you are my treasure...   Exodus 19:5
I want to establish you with all my heart and all my soul. ..Jer 32:41
And I want to show you great and marvelous things.. Jeremiah... 33:3
If you seek me with all your heart, you will find me... Deu 4:29
I am able to do more for you than you could possibly imagine... Eph3:20
For I am your greatest encourager...   2 Thessalonians 2: 16-17
I am the Father who comforts you in all your troubles... 2 Cor 1:3-4
When you are brokenhearted, I am close to you... Psalm 34: 18
One day I will wipe away every tear from your eyes... Rev 21 :3-4
And I'll take away all the pain you have suffered on this earth... Rev 21 :3-4
I am your Father, and I love you even as I love my son, Jesus.. .Jn 17:23
He came to demonstrate that I am for you, not against you...Rom8:31
And to tell you that I am not counting your sins.. .2 Cor 5: 18-19
If you receive the gift of my son Jesus you receive me... 1John 2:23
And nothing will ever separate you from my love again. Rom 8:38-39
Come home to me and I'll throw the biggest party heaven has ever
seen...Luke 15:7
I have always been your Father, and will always be your Father Eph3: 4
My question is: will you be my child?..   John 1:12-13
I am waiting for you   Luke 15: 1-32

Love, Your Dad, Almighty God

Other ways to experience this:
-have a friend read it to you & visualize that it is Jesus speaking to you.
-listen to my guided meditation CD "A Walk with Jesus" which includes Jesus reading you this letter.

"Film club"

In the book "The Film Club" David Gilmour tells how he allowed his teenaged son to drop out of school if he agreed to sit down regularly with him to watch films he selected for their life messages or artistic value. If I were to have a film club, I would include these films that would be challenging, life-affirming, inspiring or energizing: *(just to name a few!)*

Big Fish	Braveheart	Bruce Almighty	Rudy
Cinema Paradiso		Blindside	Crash
Dead Poets Society		Donnie Darko	I am Legend
Field of Dreams		7 days in Utopia	Courageous
Friday Night Lights		Ghost in a Shell 2	
Tree of Life		Signs	
Gran Torino		Invictus	
King's Speech		The Human Experience	
Les Miserables		The Apostle	
Life is Beautiful		Lion King	
Man facing Southeast		Marvin's Room	
Matrix		The Mission	
3 Burials of Melquades Estrada	On the Waterfront	
Passion of the Christ		Pay it Forward	
Rocky Balboa		Romero	
To save a Life		Up	

Five people you meet in Heaven

Mitch Albom wrote this book about the first five people you meet when you go to heaven. *My theory*: the first five people you meet in heaven are the **last** five people you want to see in heaven. If you can accept and embrace them; you're in. If not; well good luck.

For this challenging road trip make a list of who would those 5 people be for you: the last five people you think deserve to be in heaven, or that you dread the thought of spending eternity with.

That's probably the easy part.

Now pray for the ability to see them differently, to let go of the grudge if necessary; and attempt reconciliation.

Help

Look for a way to help someone or a group of people who are hurting. An Example: during the priest scandal many priests I knew encountered hatred from random people. Some even stopped going out in public in their priestly clothes. Many were depressed. I made stickers saying "We love our priests". Thousands and thousands of stickers later, many people have shared their support; helping regain respect for many good priests.

I Forgive you!

Earlier in this book, it says that perhaps the single biggest thing you could do for your spiritual life is to let go of a grudge. Don't wait another moment or day to experience this road trip.

1- Write at the top of a sheet of paper:"I forgive you"
2- Pray to God to show you who you may be holding a grudge against in any way and you need to forgive.
3- Make a list of all the people who come to mind, including not just major hurts, but also little things. Go all the way back to your childhood. Include God if you have to.
4- Go for a walk with your list, and as you walk, one at a time say their name followed by "I forgive you". Say it until you mean it and can let it go! Then move on to the next name. If there is one name or experience that you are unable to let go of; follow through with extra prayer. This could be one of the most liberating, powerful and healing experiences you will ever have.

Journal
Keep a daily journal and or scrapbook of your thoughts & ideas. Tie it in with your daily prayer & scripture and inspired reading and see what happens. Collect things that come across your daily path that move, inspire, challenge you, including the Bible.
Maybe reread this book someday & journal with it.

Lord's Prayer
The Our Father is the powerful prayer that Jesus Himself actually taught, when He was asked: "how are we supposed to pray to the Creator?". Jesus related to the Creator as "Abba" which translates most perfectly not even as Father, but "Daddy". He was trying to teach us that as old and wise as we grow; we will always need our Creator the way a child depends on their parent.

Try meditating on every single line of this prayer.

Game changers:

1- If you are in a place where at night the stars are visible, say this prayer while looking up at the heavens.

2- Imagine if the physical world were to come to an end in a way where God became visible, what should we do or say? I think we would join hands and together say the prayer that Jesus taught us.

Try saying The Lord's Prayer with a sense of all the meaning it would have as your last words in this life, or the act of humanity consecrating itself to its Creator. Really let yourself feel it. Lift up your hands toward heaven as you say "for the kingdom and the power and the glory are yours, now and forever". This could change what this prayer means to you and how you pray it from now on.

Mary

If you play or watch football no doubt you have heard the expression "a Hail Mary" pass or play. It started with Dallas Cowboys quarterback Roger Staubach in 1975. He prayed a Hail Mary right before making an incredible play. Great idea; but Mary is not just for emergencies.

Get to know and be close to Jesus' Mother. Keep a special place for her in your heart. Catholics do not worship Mary. We honor her for her special relationship with our Savior. She is a spiritual friend you do not want to be without. Check out the stories of her many apparitions around the world. With Mary it is never about herself. She serves the Creator, she serves her Son. She loves you and she wants YOU to know, love and serve her Son too.

Meditation

Meditation is a deeply powerful form of prayer. On my retreats people often say that their favorite part is the guided meditation. These guided journeys are vacations for the soul. There are many guided meditations, and you can always pick up the ones I use in my programs. You might even be inspired to create one.

Mission Statement

Every effective organization has a mission statement. It reveals what others can expect by belonging to the group, and acts as a guidepost for measuring how they are progressing.

Prayerfully create a mission statement for *your* life.

Ask: -What makes me feel most alive?

-Is there anyone I know that when I look at their life I feel "now *that's* living"?

Tip: Be strong and specific in language:

not " *I hope*" but "*I will*"   not "*I'll try to__*" but "*I do__*"

Mystery Tour

Have a day with no plans, and just go out and see what happens. Maybe visit a new town, maybe take public transportation. Bring Jesus with you. You have been created by a God who likes to surprise and amaze; be open to what He will be showing you. Go alone or with a friend who will make the most of it with you.

Nature

God's creation has an amazing ability to rejuvenate our souls. God has wired us in such a way that to be in nature lifts our spirits. So get out and explore your surroundings. Discover special places where you can find beauty and/or quiet, and can become sacred spaces; like beaches, mountains, lakes, rivers, parks, hiking trails.

Extreme:

* Grow something- having plants in your living space energizes you
* Creating and taking care of a garden gives you an experience of tending to something, and watching gradual growth happen. Things like the necessity of removing weeds, and watering all demonstrate aspects of our own lives.
* Spend a day; or if you're really adventurous a week or more, in nature- with no technology.

Oasis

Consider and live your life as a place where everyone who comes to you can find relief from the desert that daily life can become. Be an oasis, a person who others know that with you, they will be welcomed and through you loved by God. Reach out and be a friend to a misfit, an outcast.

Party

Throw a party. Be adventurous in your invitation list. Be generous, and creative with food and refreshments. Maybe have a theme. Play games. Make skits. Dance. Keep it clean. Take photos. Have fun.

Passion of the Christ
The next time you need a reminder of how much Jesus loves you, and what He went through for you, watch this movie. Forget about what you will hear about the bloodiness being over-done. Forget about the human flaws or the personal life of the director. Let yourself feel the physical passionate love of Jesus for you. And also feel the emotional passion of Mary.

Pay it forward
The concept of this worthwhile film is what every follower of Christ should be living. When a kindness is given to you; instead of paying back the person who helped you; you pay it forward. You perform a generous positive act for three random people. If they should want to pay you back; you encourage them to do what you did- pay it forward. This is how we change the world. For God so loved us, now we love each other. He invites to share in the joy of loving; of pouring it all out without concern for return.

Power prayer
Repeat this powerful prayer throughout the day:
"Jesus, Mary, I love you, save souls"

Power Songs
Sing or pray these short song verses throughout the day from your heart.
"Jesus you are, you are, everything I'm not
and everything that I'd like to be.

Jesus you are, you are, the maker of my heart
Finish what you started in me."

"Shepherd me Oh God
Beyond my wants, beyond my fears, from death into life."

Random acts of kindness

Here's a few to get you started:

* Spend some time at a store, bank or post office just opening the door for people.

* Buy a few dozen roses, and give them out to the people the Holy Spirit guides you to (usually people who look sad or stressed out).

* Make arrangements with the local funeral home or florist for them to give you the flowers they would normally be throwing out or have no use for, and find creative uses for them.

* Walk down a main street saying "good morning" or "hi" or "how you doin?" to everyone. If that seems like a bit much for you- at least smile for every person you meet.

* Play the reverse pickpocket game. Find ways to cleverly place money in strangers pockets or bags.

* Hang out in a hospital emergency room, praying for people there, and asking the Holy Spirit to show you how you might be of assistance (getting refreshments, offering tissues, a listening ear)

* On a hot summer night, in a situation where people are gathered, buy a cold watermelon and cut it up and give away slices.

* In a situation where it's hot and someone is selling ice cream, buy one for everybody in the crowd

* Pay the toll for the car behind you.
* get your friends together and give out free stuff (food, religious articles, rosaries, stickers) to people as they come out of church

Come up with your own, and *please* send them to me so we can spread them around.

Rocky Balboa
Watch this film for a good spiritual journey. Honestly I was annoyed when it was announced they were making this movie. I felt they were just doing it for the money. I thought "Rocky's old now- let it go". Then I got curious about what would the story line be. I'm thinking: "he's old; maybe he's in a nursing home. Terrorists invade the nursing home, and he beats the daylights out of them". Luckily that's not the movie they made. Rocky Balboa is not only *not* ridiculous, it's pretty inspiring. The movie doesn't mention Jesus, God or the Holy Spirit; but it is spiritually loaded. Rocky has what he calls "the fire in the basement"; another way of saying "the prompting of the Holy Spirit". It's amazing to watch how Rocky faces every situation, and see the impact he has on every person he encounters. It's a real lesson on living in the Fast Lane.

Role models
Look into a saint's life. Saints are real life spiritual role models. They had human flaws and weakness like you and I; and they gave themselves to God to become some-

thing more, in Him. Some the more interesting saints I have learned about include: *(to name a few)*

St. Anthony (OK- so I'm biased)	St. Joseph
St. Michael the Archangel	St. Francis of Assisi
St. Francis Xavier	St. Theresa Little flower
St. Teresa of Avila	St. Augustine
St. Maximilian Kolbe	St. Padre Pio
coming soon:	
St. John Paul the Great	St. Teresa of Calcutta

Share truth in love

There is a saying: "Jesus loves pagans, drunks & sinners". He does. Do you? *How can you reach out to those who might need Jesus most?* That is where he wants to be.

That's who He would be hanging out with right now. I have a friend who is into death metal music; and he loves Jesus. He has a minis- **ERADICATE ERRATIC HATE** try going where he reaches out to his peers who are into this scene. He has a band and uses the music to express messages other than the negative ones that others promote. He has a lot of guts. I respect him a lot, and I believe Jesus is with him.

These days atheism is very fashionable. There are a lot of best-selling books, Youtube videos & films promoting it. Science is always coming out with some new bit of knowledge explaining something that was once mysterious. This cultivates a sense that one day everything will be explained and we will not have any need for faith.

Some young people use atheism as a way to annoy their parents and other adults. Some use it to justify doing whatever they want without feeling guilt. Some have atheist parents and were never raised to believe in anything. Some really believe in atheism as a worldview. Many are turned off by the hypocrisy of religious people. You probably know some atheist people. You might even be one reading this.

There is no need to pick fights or start arguments with anyone. I really doubt anybody ever came to Jesus because they lost a philosophical debate. At the same time; don't be afraid to share your faith in a compassionate respectful   way. Share the *truth* in *love*. There are so many valid reasons to believe; so many aspects  of reality that reveal a Creator's intelligence. So many of the hardcore scientists, whether they study the vastness of the universe, or the smallest of particles, believe in a Creator. Once you really get deep into scientific study, the idea that everything exists randomly, becomes infinitely more absurd than believing it is intentionally created.

Be a witness to the truth with your life. Let others see the Holy Spirit is real by how you live. You motivate others to live in the *Fast Lane* by showing how alive it makes you. St. Francis of Assisi said: *"proclaim the Good news at all times. use words if necessary"*. There is nothing more powerful than the person who reveals the joy of belonging to God.

Shut Up

Make more time for quiet in your life. If you don't you will suffer two terrible handicaps:

1- you won't be able to hear the voice of God within you

2- you will lose your ability to remain centered and present in the here and now.

That is a deadly combination; and because of the overstimulation that is part of everyday life today, we are all at risk.

So this is a road trip that you should not skip and in fact should take frequently.

Spend an entire day without saying anything (including texting etc.). See what happens & what you learn. Maybe bring a journal and a Bible with you. Tie in an experience of Adoration for an extra bonus.

Have a totally tech-free day. Unplug yourself, spend a whole day with no technology- no TV, smart phone, computer, video games, ipod- nothing. See what happens; what it brings out in you, and what you learn. It's a great way to help you put everything into perspective, and also to find out if you are addicted.

Six Word Memoir

If you had to write the story of your life as it was, is and as you hope it to be, in six words or less what would you say? What words, impulses, visions, themes, experiences, thoughts, feelings, emotions, memories, dreams, desires, losses, hurts, perceptions, fears, and associations would you express within those few words or sentence?

Sloppy

If I ever have a meltdown, I don't think it will be from the almost 500 retreat and events a year that I do. It will be from dealing with the traffic getting to and from those events! I was recently crawling in rush hour traffic on the Long Island Expressway heading to an evening retreat, and I saw flashing cop car lights in my mirror. I was hardly moving, and I'm wondering what could he possibly be pulling me over for. I was told that I had changed lanes without using my directionals.

My first reaction is "and you have nothing else to do tonight; besides bother me about that". Luckily I was able to keep that thought in my head without it coming out of my mouth. As I continued along the trip, I started to watch myself driving, and I realized that I had gotten sloppy. Sometimes I would switch lanes and use the directionals, and sometimes I would just scoot over and not bother. Getting the ticket made me realize I needed to clean up my act.

Here's your road trip. Step back and take an observer role in your life for awhile. Ask the Holy Spirit to show you any areas of your life you may have gotten sloppy in. Pray for the ability to see and catch yourself as you continue to grow.

Spiritual "Bucket List"
Set yourself some goals of spiritual experiences for your life and make your own spiritual Bucket List.
Some possible ideas:

*the road trips in this book
*make a pilgrimage to a shrine, apparition site, or holy place like the Holy Land
*create and conduct a retreat or spiritual event
*get involved sharing your faith with those younger
* create or watch a spiritual movie

Spiritual Direction

A spiritual director is someone who can help you understand how the Holy Spirit is working in your life. A guide who can help your spiritual growth by realizing the spiritual messages to be gained through the experiences of your life. Some people like to have one director that visit on a regular basis. Some have several people they can talk with informally or occasionally about the journey of their soul.

Spiritual Warfare

Every act of love, and every prayer offered up diminishes the strength of evil in this world. Be more consciously involved in doing all you can by anchoring your life in Christ.
* Lift up Hail Marys to Our Blessed Mother all day long. Each one you offer up is ammunition in her war against the evil one.
* Say this prayer:

Saint Michael the Archangel,
defend us in battle.
Be our protection against the wickedness and snares of the devil.
May God rebuke him, we humbly pray;
and do Thou, O Prince of the Heavenly Host -
by the Divine Power of God -
cast into hell, satan and all the evil spirits,
who roam throughout the world seeking the ruin of souls. Amen.

Spread the Good News

People these days need the Good News. Many are lost and searching, and many of your generation were raised by parents with no faith. They have never been taught about Jesus, and about their destiny to live life beyond the animal state of the slow and middle lanes. They have no idea how to live a life full of the Holy Spirit in the *Fast Lane*. Let your witness be your main way of sharing the Good News; but don't be afraid to speak up if necessary.

-Who do you know well, that you're pretty sure never got taught about God?

-How can you witness to them?

-Who can you pray for now, and from now on; putting them in the hands of Jesus, the Good Shepherd, who saves the lost sheep?

-What experience or group could you bring them to?

-What might you be able to put in their hands that could open them up to God's love for them and meeting Jesus?

Stand up

Make a stand for what's right and stand with those who struggle and suffer. Many people today are in a great depression because we know how people are suffering and yet we do nothing. If you don't know; **educate yourself** about what's going on in the world:

*1 in 4 babies are murdered in Abortion

*1 in 8 humans go to bed hungry at night

*1 in 100 Americans are in jail

*36,000 children die every day of starvation & disease

*40% of American teens self mutilate

* 1 in 100 teens have an eating disorder
* there is a devastation of the oceans, the environment, & many species of life
* there is increasing economic injustice, exploitation of people, and a systematic obliteration of human rights
* militarism is a plague across the planet
* slavery & human trafficking are growing
                    These are just to name a few

Use the internet to learn about these issues. Read. Watch documentary films & programs. Increase your awareness, and motivate others to take action.

Most of all, be an instrument of Grace and *take some action*. Ask the Holy Spirit about what *you* can and should do personally. Pray about ***what is it that Jesus wants you do do*** about the problems in the world; otherwise it will all be too overwhelming. If you are doing what God wants you to do, then you will have peace. Remember that it is so much more important to be faithful than successful.

Walk around the block

Get out and play! Travel the streets of your town. Visit a new church. Stop in at a new place. Check out parts of town you never get to. Ask God to bless every single person you meet or pass. Smile at everyone.

the main thing is to keep the main thing the main thing

conclusion

Remember: the main thing is that we are all going home somewhere.
No one gets to live here forever.

At the end of your life will Jesus see Himself in you or not?

I pray that something I said here in this book will inspire you to live the kind of life that the answer to that question will be "YES!" The *Fast Lane* life of holiness and sainthood, of oneness with God; living for Him and with Him is not something just for the few. YOU were made by the Creator for this privilege; this pilgrimage of striving humbly, heroically to live a godly, authentic, noble life.
YOU WERE BORN FOR THIS ADVENTURE OF A LIFE IN THE *FAST LANE*!

Thank you for taking the time to read this book. I hope it will make a difference in your life, and in the lives of those you love.
I don't say goodbye, I say
"see you later!"
If I don't get to meet you or
see you again in this life,
we'll party in the next.
vaya con dios   Tony

Remember: I am with you always until the end of the age.   *-Jesus*

Notes

It's The End of the world as we know it!

 If you should be alive during an apocalyptic event re-member: Pray and love and anchor yourself in Jesus & Mary.

This book is just an introduction, a starting point, a foundation. While what I presented here could probably keep you busy for a lifetime there is more to the path. In the sequel there will be many more insights, stories, and road trips I want to share for you to build on the foundation this book lays out. It will also include: *the second greatest story (N)ever told.*

If there is anything you would like to see included let me know.

Maybe you can help:
* Translating this book into other languages
* Please help me put these books in the hands of as many young people as possible through every high school, youth ministry, parish, and juvenile prison ministry in the world by sending me your connections.

A summary of life in the Fast Lane:

-Open the door of your heart to God and accept His love.

-Follow God by loving Him in return by loving others

-Stay hungry for a deeper, fuller life.

-Let go of false ways of being in control.

-Accept that as a human being, you are not, and are not meant to be, in control- God is.

-How you label yourself and your life will determine how you live.

-More than anything, see yourself as a man or woman of God

-Let your weakest links; sin and pain, be the open door to God for his mercy & healing.

-Let God heal you: directly, through those you trust, through counselors if needed.

-Appreciate everything as gifts from God: the beauty of creation, those that love you with no conditions, joyful moments, miraculous occurrences.

-Be a giver, not a taker, & give generously the way God does.

-Live passionately; love without limit. Avoid laziness, procrastination.

-Discipline yourself to resist temptation, addiction.

-Deal with your emotional issues of anger, fear, and pain.

-Be vigilant against and avoid: isolation, judgement, jealousy, pride, selfishness

-Do not give into despair or peer pressure

-Read the Bible, especially the Gospels

-Pay attention to your conscience telling you when you have gone against God. Confess your sins

-Know and follow God's code for us (Commandments & Beatitudes).

-Anchor your life in faith, hope and love.

-Pray constantly. Worship God regularly through Holy Mass, meditation and adoration.

-Stay alive in the moment, and remember to trust. God often works in mysterious ways.

-Remember that change in life is possible; but almost never easy.

-Maintain an attitude of gratitude and be responsible for the gifts you have been given.

-Extend forgiveness and mercy to others. Let go of grudges.

-Fast and sacrifice often.

-Maintain integrity and be faithful in small things.

-Let Jesus lead you. Accept His will in your life and put your actions in His hands.

-Stay connected to a community of believers.

-Dream big, follow your spiritual passion, and never give up on what God has placed in your heart.

-Create more, consume less. Live simply.

-Stay connected to your spiritual friends in heaven, especially Mary.

-Remember that no prayer or act of love is wasted.

-Keep a sense of humor and have as much fun as possible.

-Treasure and cultivate your relationships.

-Creating and experiencing art energizes your soul.

-Spread the Good News so others may experience your joy.

about the author

Tony Bellizzi is a retreat director, youth minister and prison minster and conducts nearly 500 events a year. He has shared the Good News of God's Love for 40 years in churches, schools, jails, locker-rooms, bars, bingo halls, football fields, streets and country clubs. He has witnessed throughout the United States, and on almost every continent.

Tony has spoken at Diocesan, Regional and parish Youth Rallies, parish missions, Confirmation and Graduation retreats, at middle schools, high schools, universities; for students, faculties, and parents.

He attended SUNY Old Westbury, and also holds masters degrees from The Seminary of the Immaculate Conception- (Theology) and Bankstreet College of Education- (Educational Supervision & Administration).

Tony is the founder and director of Hope for the Children Foundation, a not-for-profit organization committed to peace and justice by empowering those most in need. He is the subject of the documentary films "The Vault" & "Hope for the Children". Tony appears as himself in the films: "City of Eternal Spring" and "The Human Experience".

Tony is also a performance artist; creating and performing numerous one-man shows. He directs "The Vault" an underground performance scene in NYC; and produces "Soul Fountain" art & literary journal.

When not on the road, Tony lives in Queens Village NYC, on Facebook, & online @ retreets@aol.com
& HopeForTheChildren.org

Brand New from Tony Bellizzi:

Full of Grace
The second greatest story (n)ever told
an exploration of the apparitions of the Virgin Mary

*Dare

A common sense and spiritual method for facing life's challenges. Tony offers advice and a comprehensive approach for dealing with the major issues affecting todays teens.

*Living Bread
A concise record of the Eucharistic Miracles.

All three new books are available at Amazon.com or from Tony directly

The Fast Lane- *the adventure of a lifetime*

Order Form   *amounts are suggested donations to Hope for the Children Foundation, which receives all proceeds & includes postage*

Books $12.00 each   ___The Fast Lane
        $10 .00 each   ___Full of Grace
        $10.00 each   ___Dare
        #10.00 each   ___Living Bread

Guided meditation CD's $10.00 each
___Journey with Jesus
___A Walk with Jesus (Beach)
___A Special time with Jesus & Mary

___Rosary bracelets $2.00

___Rosaries (Free)__with instructions__no instructions
mail with Check made out to "Hope for the Children"
      9021 Springfield Blvd.   Queens Village NY 11428

Name_____

Address _____

City,State,Zip_____

Tony is available for retreats and spiritual growth experiences   718-479-2594

Youth
Confirmation retreats
Graduation retreats
Youth rallies
Youth ministry group meetings
Bullying and violence prevention programs
Leadership & Peer ministry training

Adults
Parish missions and retreats
Parents presentations
Mens Spirituality
Prayer Groups
Communion Breakfasts
Faculty and Catechist retreats

All Ages
Family catechesis Programs
"Full of Grace"- apparitions of Mary
"Living Bread" Eucharistic Miracles